DREAM...

a guide to grieving gracefully

With 5 Keys to
Unlock the Grip of Grief

Kristi Smith

Kristi R. Smith

ISBN: 978-0692595886

Printed in the United States of America

Photo Credit:
Abigail Wensyel,
www.abbiwensyelphotography.com

Printed by:

www.AbundantPress.com

To Receive Additional

Videos and Other Resources,

Register This Book at:

KristiSmithDreamBook.com

"Kristi's book DREAM is wonderful, wonderful, wonderful! Her method of using keys to unlock each stage of grief is easy to comprehend and beautifully written. A master storyteller, Kristi envelopes the bereaved with compassion and comfort in a pintsize book that fits perfectly in our hands and heart. A true gem that should be on the nightstand of every griever."

-Lynda Cheldelin Fell, President of the National Grief & Hope Coalition

"Kristi has inspired me as she has shared her authentic journey through the dark valley of grief. She is a beautiful tour guide through terrible terrain, sharing stories and insights that will give great hope to those who must walk this path."

-Nicole Johnson, Author of "Fresh Brewed Life" and Dramatist with Women of Faith

"In her book "Dream", Kristi not only invites you on a journey of heartfelt transparency and grace, but she puts an arm around your shoulder and walks with you every step of the way. She has taken the most personal heartbreak of her life and made it a ministry to those grieving. What a beautiful act of love and redemption."

-Melissa Maimone, Christian Speaker & Writer

"Kristi is the REAL deal! Authentic, compassionate, and vibrant - she is truly an inspiration. Our support group loved her and her powerful message!"

-Pam Walker, Co-Founder, Young Widows Support Group, Dayton, Ohio

"As a human being who has experienced much loss there are few books that speak to my soul. Kristi's book takes you from hopeless to living freely again. With truth, experience and faith, you could not be in better hands."
-Angie Cartwright, Motivational speaker and Founder of National Grief Awareness Day

"I am so proud of Kristi for taking an enormous loss and encouraging others that there is hope and healing amid the grief. Kristi inspires how critical it is that we must walk through the tornado of pain in order to find complete peace, hope and freedom."
-Tanya Brown, Sister of Nicole Brown Simpson, Celebrity Keynote Speaker and Author of "Finding Peace Amid The Chaos: My Escape From Depression and Suicide" and "Seven Characters of Abuse: Domestic Violence, Where It Starts and Where It Can End"

"I had the pleasure of connecting with Kristi through social media. While many people shy away from Facebook, Twitter and other similar formats, God uses these outlets to connect and inspire His people, which is what He did for my sister and I. Through Kristi's writings and passion to uplift the hurting, I'm encouraged to keep dreaming BIG no matter how difficult life becomes. She has been a beautiful blessing to my life and my ministry. "
-Rhovonda L. Brown, Founder & Executive Director of Martha & Mary Ministries, Walking in Freedom! And author of bestselling book "Walking in Freedom! A Thirty-Day Devotional Journey for Women"

Dedication

This collection of life lessons is, first and foremost, dedicated to God for His graciousness to me; to Jesus for giving His own life so that I can have life eternal in Him; and to the Spirit, who continues to comfort and guide me. From one wild, wide-eyed widow to the God who continues to hold me and heal me, thank You. I would be hopeless without You. I am secure forever in Your unending love.

This book is dedicated, in loving memory of Michael James Smith, to our beautiful daughters.

Faith Erin Smith: your name means "secure faith, solid assurance, and confident expectation." You inspire me to be bolder and chase after my dreams. Thank you for your compassion and example of living faith and for sharing the gift of your strong spirit with me. My sincere gratitude for your many, many hours of typing this book - you are the sweetest scribe ever. You poured your heart into this with me and I am truly grateful. May the words you transcribed be written in your heart so that you may continue to have bold faith in God and the dreams He has for you. You amaze me. You are one strong woman! I love to see you discovering your passion and pursuing your dreams with no fear. God has put such a spark in you.

Shine bright, my little ginger—no dimming necessary.

Abigail Joy Wensyel: your first name means "your father's joy" and alongside your middle name, you are "double joy." Thank you for living your life with creativity and zeal and sharing your outrageous joy with me. Your heart's lens captures hidden glories. You captured the essence of our journey of grief in your photo of the tree growing out of a rock. I am honored to use this as the cover photo for the book. Abigail, may your roots go down deep into the solid foundation of your Father's love and may your branches reach high into the glorious grace of your father's joy. I want to thank you for your love and constant support. You have been a role model of how to weather a severe loss and hold onto joy. I delight to see you moving forward in your faith and pursuing your dream of owning your own photography business to live out your God-given destiny.

Faith and Abigail, your father adored you and your mother delights in you. Continue to Dare to Dream, my daughters. I love you both dearly. — Mama

A special thanks to all the wonderful people at the K-LOVE radio station: I have literally had your station on since my husband died and your content has been a constant source of strength for me. I crank up the songs during the day in the house, I listen in the car, and I keep your station on low in the house at night.

I even leave it on when I am not home just so it fills the air with good energy. Countless times your songs and Encouraging Word of the Day have lifted my spirit.

Thank you for keeping it positive and encouraging—I have felt the LOVE from K-LOVE.

And last, but not least; a heartfelt thanks to Lisa McClurg. She helped me tear this book apart and put it back together again. With her help, I have communicated as clearly as possible how DREAMers can grieve gracefully and dare to DREAM. I could not have taken this book to the next level without you. You are an answered prayer.

Dear DREAMers

You may think that "DREAM" is an unusual title for a book designed to help with grief, but I propose that DREAMing is precisely the right antidote for our aching hearts. DREAM is an acronym for a five-step process to neutralize the stages of grief and release the power to heal.

Each of the five stages of grief is paired with specific keys to unlock the pain of grief and unleash the energy to heal. This book contains practical steps that are designed to increase your capacity to fully live, even in the face of loss. In this guide to grieving gracefully, I share insights and examples that will help you learn to dare to dream. We all, as grievers, need to learn to navigate through loss and into the fullness of life again. Sometimes we just need to know how to do it, and how to do it gracefully.

You have a choice to make: you can get caught in the anger and sadness of grief or you can learn to process these necessary emotions and use the discoveries made in these low places to catapult yourself into renewed living. DREAM helps the grief-stricken turn their pain into gained experiences for propelling their lives forward with dignity, strength and grace. Chapter One of your life is punctuated by grief. Chapter Two begins by turning the page and allowing grief to grant you gifts that empower you to go on living. There is life after grief. Your life. Make it extraordinary.

Grief…Friend or Foe?

Grief itself is a neutral entity, neither friend nor foe. Grief only has the power that we give it. Grief has the power to heal, fill and give new life or the power to debilitate, confine, and condemn. The choice is up to the griever. Grief can be your friend or your enemy. It all depends on you. Many times, we as grievers do not know how to harness the power for good. Our good. Ultimate good. We end up being more hurt in the process. In reality, if we knew better, we could use the power of grief to not only heal ourselves, but to help those around us, too.

I believe that grief can be a gift and that grieving can bring us gifts. I know this will take some contemplation and examination before you are able to believe this. All I ask is that you give equal opportunity to explore both possibilities of grief. Open your mind to the dual ideas of what grief can do and in the end you will be able to make a more informed decision about the power of grief in your own life. Deal? Deal!

Wisdom from Hydrangeas

Hydrangeas are my favorite flower—I love the big glorious blooms. When we added the patio on the back of our house, I only had one request…hydrangeas. So the landscape specialist dug down deep into the hard rock soil and created beds for them.

Rich soil was laid and small hydrangea bushes were planted on the lakeside of our newly laid patio.

I asked the landscaper if there were any special instructions for this type of flower. He gave me two things to remember: make sure they stay watered and cut them back every spring. "How much do I trim them?" I asked. He said, "Cut them back to about two feet high." Low maintenance beauty. Perfect.

Hydrangeas are a midsummer bloomer. A late bloomer. I like that. I am, too. That first year the plants were beautiful. They were covered in large, white heads that gently aged to a celery green and eventually turned a caramel color by late fall. The leaves would fall during the autumn, but the blooms would stay all winter long. So even during the bleak gray of winter they stood tall with their regal heads held high.

When that first spring approached, I was apprehensive to chop these beauties back to two feet. They had reached well over five feet tall and I was afraid to cut them in half. Wouldn't that kill them? I remembered the advice from the professional landscaper and followed his instructions. I have to be honest. It was difficult to do. I felt like I was massacring my grand beauties. Surely they would not endure such harsh treatment. When I was done cutting them back, all the remnants of softness were gone. All that remained were five short shrubs of sticks. They looked pitiful. Perhaps I had gone too far and killed them.

How would they ever come back after such a severe pruning?

3

Time Will Tell

So I waited: time would tell. I held onto what the landscaper had said and tried to believe I had done the right thing. That first spring was the longest. Every so often I would peer out of my upstairs window overlooking the patio and say a little prayer for my hydrangea bushes to pull through.

There was not much sign of growth for about a month or more after the pruning. Then, the butchered sticks started to send off new shoots, little bursts of bright green came out of the blunt gray wood. Spring was in full bloom everywhere else I looked with brilliant green grass. The trees were budding, and then blooming. Pops of color were all around. Yellows, pinks, purples. My hydrangea bushes did not keep up with the rest of nature bursting forth all around us. They looked more like mangled firewood at this point.

Spring gave way to summer and my hydrangeas were growing taller and sprouting leaves. No blooms yet, but I was glad to see that I had not completely annihilated these lovelies. When the 4th of July came and went, I started to panic because there were still no blooms. But, soon after that there appeared to be buds on the top of the tall stems. Finally on my birthday, in the third week of July, they had started to bloom.

Relief and happiness bloomed in my heart at the sight of these long-awaited flowers.

White, fluffy, and gloriously grand, these beauties were taller than me. Reaching my hands toward the sky I could not even touch the heads of these towering flower heads. There were five bushes in a row against the back of our patio and they made a magnificent hedge of hydrangeas.

Every year, I go through the same hesitation to cut them back in the spring. For almost ten years now I've done it anyway, and every year they have gotten fuller and taller and more breathtaking than the year before.

Deep Pruning

Maybe you can relate to the severe trimming that my garden plants endured. It is possible that you also withstood a deep pruning in your life. Do you remember a time when there seemed to be more cut away than remained? Perhaps you have felt like a mangled pile of sticks and questioned your ability to ever spring back. Grief is like a deep pruning of the soul.

Be encouraged by my hardy hydrangeas. You will also come back stronger, more vibrant, and standing a little taller.

Do not be discouraged by the other people you witness blooming around you. Grief is a late bloomer, but it will yield a glorious bouquet of beauty when it does.

Late Bloomer

God has not allowed you to be cut back more than you can withstand. Growth will happen, slowly but surely. Be patient with yourself. Keep reaching up toward heaven. Simultaneously dig down deep into the soil of your soul and find the strength you need hidden there.

5

Learn from my hydrangeas: be encouraged by their beauty and resilience. You are more precious than these to your Creator.

The Master Gardener has His eyes on you and He will not allow this painful pruning to destroy you. Trust God to know how to help you grow. He will water your dry earth, shine on your tender growth, and help you to eventually stand tall and strong. You will bloom! It is what you are made to do!

Loss and Longing

You might be grieving over a death, a divorce, a job loss, loss of health, or any number of other losses. We grieve losses, but you may also be grieving from a longing; longing for a child, a spouse, financial security, or a better relationship with family members. Loss and longing are both forms of grief.

Infertility is a struggle that so many people face. The struggle is real. Each month that conception does not happen, the couple is faced with their grief. There are alternative ways to have children, but even if the couple chooses to adopt, they will be healthier if they have grieved having children naturally. Grieving is an important part of making peace with your life. Don't rush on to the next fix without giving yourself time to heal.

Different for Everyone

Grief can be fierce and overwhelming, or subtle and mysterious. Grieving is a tricky process. I hope my suggestions help you navigate through the grieving process, but I am also aware that grieving is a delicate, personal, and intricate journey. Depending on our circumstances, our support structure, and our ability to deal with our emotions, grieving will look different for each one of us.

Grieving is the strange and mystical process of letting go of someone or something we held dear to us. Your grief will look different from mine. I am writing from my own personal encounter with grief, which is that of a widow with two daughters. I am grieving with my own set of challenges and strengths. What I intend to do is call on the common elements of grief and learn from them. There are some common aspects of grieving and I will focus on those. These ideas are not written as a rulebook, but more like a collection of suggestions.

Grieving is not an exact science. I am a creative type, so feel free to be creative with the suggestions offered here. Come up with your own recipe.

Hold onto the ingredients that you like and that serve your life and let go of the others. Customize your own grief process. The things written here are for your evaluation, and are offered only as an aid to your personal grief process.

Try to hear these offerings as my own learnings from my specific situation. The idea is that these writings may spark healing within your own set of circumstances. I speak to you on a more universal level of grief and do not presume to know your personal loss.

I do not pretend to know the pain of losing a child, or watching a parent die, or the separation

7

and anxiety of going through a divorce. But please do not hear me talking down to you. It is my humble hope that something I say in these pages will help you be able to lift the veil of grief and sadness, even if just the slightest bit.

Grief moves at its own speed, but there are things we can do to help the process keep moving along. Conversely, there are things that we can do that can keep us from moving forward toward healing. Our actions do play a role in the overall speed and direction of the grieving process. It is important to pace yourself. Grief is not a 100-yard dash and there are no awards given out for speed. Grief is more like a marathon, so it is critical that you approach it with that in mind. Pace yourself, but keep moving forward.

Grief is not a competitive sport. You will do yourself a lot of harm by comparing yourself to others and how they are grieving.

Don't define your success or failure that way: that could prove deadly.

Do your own personal best and encourage your fellow grievers along the way. We are all in this together.

Radical Measures

Although grief is basically an emotional process, there are practical elements and specific behaviors that play an important role in the emotional healing. It is vital for you to know ahead of time that these actions will not feel natural at the time, and they will certainly not feel comfortable. They may seem radical and uncalled for, but consider the suggestions prayerfully.

There are some pretty radical measures we are called to carry out when healing is the goal. In the medical world, patients submit to medications, therapy, surgery, and even more extreme measures in the hopes of healing. The same is true in the emotional world, especially when it comes to grief. There are some things you may need to do in the grieving process that would seem extreme in any other setting, but may be perfectly appropriate for this time and this situation.

This process may require you to do some things that would seem out of the ordinary under different circumstances. It is important to be thoughtful and reflective before taking radical actions, but don't let fears keep you from doing what you need to do to heal.

Listen to the advice of wise counsel, but in the end know that it is your life and you are allowed to make whatever choices you deem necessary and life giving.

For example, women love their hair. We spend time and money to cut, color, and style it. It is not natural for our hair to fall out, and normally we would fight to keep it. However, we willingly submit to take a drug that causes our hair to fall out for the greater good of fighting the life threatening disease of cancer.

Grief makes us do real emotional work. In order to heal, we have to do uncomfortable things. Sometimes, what we must do to heal is downright scary. That is why it is important to keep in mind the end result: healing. In the healing process, things may get worse before they get better. Don't worry. Our goal is learning to grieve so we can heal. You are moving in the right direction. Stay with me.

Grieving Gracefully

I am a creative type person. My husband used to lovingly call me "artsy-fartsy." My mind automatically searches for creative solutions to everyday problems. When I was suddenly thrust into the grieving process, my mind again began searching for creative solutions to this very concrete problem of how to grieve. When I asked myself how to grieve, and creatively grieve, the answer I heard unfolded before me in pieces— fragments, really. In time, I have been able to put them all together and this is my attempt to share these creative insights with you.

Grief is radically different than I ever thought it would be. We can't predict how we will respond to something until it happens. Grief took my breath away. I am learning to breathe again. Grief itself is a raw, awkward, and vulnerable experience. Grief requires you to take seemingly unnatural steps in order to move through the pain.

What I learned was that grief is different for every person going through it. Grief is as different as the people who are grieving. It is very personal and individual. Grief is not a "one size fits all" garment. I won't pretend to tell anyone else how to grieve—that would be disastrous. What I intend to do is to call on the common elements of grief and learn from those. There are some common aspects of grieving and I will focus on those.

The only ways I have found to "grieve gracefully" have challenged me to the depths of my person. Grief has made me call on undeveloped parts of my character and bring them into the light. Grief has stretched my body, heart, mind, and soul in ways that nothing else ever has or will. Grief has made me deal with issues I have buried and long forgotten. Grief has made me wrestle with a darkness and aloneness I did not know existed. Grief is meant to shake us to the very core of our existence in order to bring a whole new way of being into our life.

Compassion

There is no way I can speak directly to your pain and sorrow. All I can do is share insights from my own personal experience and hope to inspire you to search for your own recovery path. If at any point you feel I am making grief sound too simple, too easy to manage, or too generic for your situation, I would ask you to know that I am indeed sorry for your specific loss. Even if you feel that I have no idea what you have been through, no concern for your deep hurt, or no real understanding for the depths of your pain, please remember that I am writing these things to you to help in any way I can. If you only receive one tip from me on how to wrestle with the monster of grief, then I ask you to receive it as a gift with my most heartfelt compassion.

No Magic Wand

These pages are not written from extensive research that was compiled over years, or from a doctor's or counselor's perspective. This book is not even coming from a person well versed in the fine art of grief recovery. This is my healing heart reaching out to your hurting heart and saying I am

11

sorrowful you are hurting. Grief sucks! I wish I could wave a magic wand and make all the pain go away. There were many times I wished I could just wake up from this nightmare to find it was all a bad dream. However, there is no magic wand and it wasn't just a bad dream, so I offer you what I can...my lessons, my learnings, and my love. This is just me, a widow, writing to you with hopes that in this process of writing and reading we will both be led to healing and wholeness.

Why Grieve?

In the first year after Mike died, I encountered hundreds of people who were stuck in grief, and living in perpetual pain. Even as a new griever, I instinctively knew there was something wrong. It scared me and made me ask, "Why aren't they healing? Am I going to heal? Or am I going to get stuck in this same death trap?" Loss and longing, if not addressed and healed, can be very destructive both to the grievers and to those around them. Although it is often unintentional, brokenness causes more brokenness. Millions of people are hurting because they don't know how to heal.

Most people think of grieving like going into a deep, dark endless cave. They avoid the grieving because they feel they will get lost in that cave and never be able to get out. There will be dark times, but it's important to realize that grief is not a deep, dark endless cave. Instead, picture it as a tunnel with a bright light at the end. That light illuminates the passageway no matter how dark it feels.

In an attempt to avoid the hurt, they avoid grieving. In reality, grieving is the process that leads to healing. The only reason to grieve is to heal. This book maps out that path through grief and into healing.

Grieving is a necessary, though unpleasant, part of life. At some point or points in all of our lives, we will have to grieve the loss of someone we love, or the longing for something we want. The statistics below indicate a grief problem of epidemic proportion. The magnitude of loss is staggering. These statistics demand our attention:

- 8 million people suffered through the death of someone in their immediate family (National Mental Health Association)
- 800,000 widows and widowers (National Mental Health Association)
- 400,000 people under 25 suffered from the death of a loved one (National Mental Health Association)
- 1.2M children will lose a parent to death before age 15 (Dr. Elizabeth Weller, Dir. Ohio State University Hospitals, 1991)
- 1.9M youngsters under age 18 have lost one or both parents. (U. S. Social Security Administration)
- Each year in the United States nearly 26,000 babies are stillborn. (www.stopstillbirthasap.org)
- Every 78 seconds a teen attempts suicide. Every 90 seconds they succeed. (National Center for Health Statistics)
- 1 in 7 Americans lose a parent or sibling before age 20. 1/3 of Americans who lost a sibling

13

believe their family never recovered from the loss. (www.disabled-world.com)

- 1 in 5 bereaved persons is likely to develop a psychiatric disorder. The highest rate is found in boys. (Journal of Child Psychology, Oct. 2000)

- In a survey of 300 incarcerated teens, 96% indicated that someone significant in their lives had died. (Columbia University)

- 85% of all prisoners on death row experienced the death of a parent during their childhood. (Virginia Simpson PHD, The Mourning Star Center, CA)

- 60% of those who lose a spouse or significant other will experience a serious illness in the 12 months following that loss. (www.widowshope.org/kids-hope/children-and-grief/)

- There is one divorce in America approximately every 36 seconds. 2,400 divorces per day. 16,800 divorces per week. 876,000 divorces a year. (usa.gov/1dMPvI2)

- Children of divorced parents are seven times more likely to suffer from depression in adult life than people of similar age and background whose parents have not divorced. (griefspeaks.com)

- 6.7 million women ages 15-44 struggle with infertility (ability to get pregnant or carry a baby to term) (www.cdc.gov)

These are grim statistics. Grief is universal. If you are human, you will grieve at some point in your life. Here is what I have found to be true. Hurt is a given; healing is not. The problem is that we really don't know how to grieve. It's a life skill that we are simply not taught. What if there was a book that could teach people how to grieve?

The Good News

DREAM is a "how to" book for the millions of people who are hurting because they don't know how to heal. DREAM is about so much more than survival. DREAM is a new way of living. If you are currently processing a loss or longing, or if you have old grief that needs additional healing, it is my hope that you will Dare to DREAM!

This little book is packed with wisdom and the all-important life skills you will need to help you pass the hardest tests you will face. DREAM is not all about the trauma and tragedy of my story. DREAM is about hope and how to infuse energy and victory into your story. I want you to start believing that growth can happen even in the hard places. When you think of whatever it is you are facing right now, I want you to put the word DREAM right beside it. Dare to DREAM! Your life is waiting for you.

Grieve Together

Let this be a time when you lean into each other as family and friends to comfort one another. Hear the pain in each other's voices, see the grief in each other's eyes, and feel it in each other's hugs. Lean in and hold on together. Allow each other's pain to actually comfort one another. Grief can strengthen a relationship or tear it apart. Hurt together, not apart.

15

My husband Mike's family—consisting of his dad, mom, brother, sisters, nieces, and nephews—were a great comfort to the girls and I even though they were also grieving. His mom and dad had known Mike his whole life, obviously, and yet they were a comfort to us as we also comforted them. Mike's sisters and brother, who were broken-hearted over the death of their brother, were so supportive to the girls and me.

In the case of death, sometimes we end up burying much more than just the person who died. We may also bury our dreams, our futures, our families, our happiness, our potential. We may even unknowingly bury ourselves. This is a tragedy beyond reality, but I have seen it time and time again. It doesn't need to be this way. Grieving is a hard process, but NOT grieving is even harder. In a sense, when you refuse to grieve, deny the pain and stuff the feelings, you don't heal. The only way to live is to grieve.

There is so much potential for confusion in this early stage of grief. We can end up losing much more than the person who died.

It may seem outrageous to say this, but I think it must be said again: DON'T BURY THE LIVING WITH THE DEAD.

Here is an example of burying the living with the dead: a father passes away and the kids feel as if they've lost their mother at the same time. In essence, the mother buried herself with the father, and the children must grieve the loss of both parents. They were orphaned by the mother's inability to live without the father. The irony is the mother is still very much alive physically, but dead on the inside.

The inability to grieve has robbed many families of years of interactions and memories. Grief has overwhelmed them, and left them for dead. There has already been enough lost, we don't need to compound it. That is why I believe it is absolutely vital to learn how to grieve. Otherwise, we end up burying much more than the dead. We bury the living with the dead.

Blinded by Grief

An interesting story of grief is found in Genesis 37 when Jacob, the father of many children, is confronted with the supposed death of his favorite son Joseph. Jacob refuses to be comforted. He even goes as far as to say he will continue to mourn until he joins his son in the grave. All of his sons and daughters came to comfort him, but this father continued to push their love away. In essence, Jacob was saying he had nothing to live for. It didn't matter that he had other children relying on him.

Was Jacob really intending to let his whole family be lost to the grief of one son? What about the rest of the children? What were they to do if their father refused to comfort them or to be comforted by them? I don't want to sound cold, but this is bad math. Even logically, it would not make sense for Jacob to give up living, because he had so much to live for.

Jacob was blinded by grief. Not literally blind as in he could not see with his eyes, but emotionally blind. Jacob could not see his own flesh and blood standing before him, because his grief blinded him to their pain. He could only see his own pain.

17

Jacob stubbornly refused to be comforted and this put the entire family at risk.

Jacob was as good as dead to the remaining children. He gave the loss of someone he dearly loved the additional power to undo his whole family. Death takes the dead, but we must refuse to allow death the power to take the living, too.

This is why grieving is essential not only to your health, but also to the health of your family. Allow yourself to be comforted - don't refuse comfort when it is offered. You are not only hurting yourself, but also hurting your family. Not consciously hurting your family, but still hurting them nonetheless. Grief already hurts so much. Do not add unnecessary pain by refusing to be consoled.

Let's make sure that we hold onto the living, even as we grieve the dead. Grief can be blinding. It can blind us to so many things. God does not want us to be blinded by grief. He wants us to be able to see and appreciate those treasures we have around us.

So let's be clear...what do we bury? What are we careful not to bury?

Bury the dead. Don't bury the living.
Bury the past. Don't bury the future.
Bury the person. Don't bury the personality.
Bury the body. Don't bury the spirit.
Bury the teacher. Don't bury the lessons learned.
Bury the lover. Don't bury the love shared.
Bury the leader. Don't bury the leadings.
Bury the fighter. Don't bury the fight.
Bury the dreamer. Don't bury the dream.
Bury the family member. Don't bury the whole family.
Bury yesterday. Don't bury today.
Bury what was. Don't bury what can be.

One Step at a Time

How do we grieve? How do we accept what has happened and move through the stages of grief to take hold of hope and healing? How do we loosen the grip of grief and claim the gifts contained inside? The actual process of grieving has five steps: denial, anger, sadness, bargaining, and acceptance. In order to move from denial to acceptance, we must pass through our emotions. It is important to feel the feelings along the way, but equally as important not to get stuck in them. It is healthy to feel sad over the loss of a loved one, but it is not healthy to get stuck feeling profoundly sad for the rest of your life.

Grieving is meant to be a step-by-step process with each step bringing us closer to healing. We walk towards wholeness on one continual path. This book is meant to give you stepping-stones through the grief process. When you find yourself ready to move on to the next step of grieving, you will be guided from one to the next. It will take time, but rest assured that you can get there. Healing happens in stages just like grief happens in stages. Step boldly forward, confident that you will be met with what you need at each step of the way.

Give yourself time at each stepping-stone to feel the feelings and bring the healing. The alternative is to stop the healing. You have probably met someone who is caught on the sad step. They have not been able to move on. Perhaps you have someone you know who is trapped in the anger stage. They are angry about everything. It is important to get mad about what you have lost, but you don't want to stay mad. That would be madness.

Climbing Higher

Stay with me as we travel through the grieving stages. Picture this as a backpacking trip, not a camping trip. Along the path, we will set up temporary camp for a season, but we aren't going to make a permanent camp. We will keep venturing forward, because we have a goal in mind. We want to reach the top step of acceptance.

Each step brings us higher and closer to healing. Climbing up out of the valley, we will scale higher until we reach the top. When we reach the pinnacle, we will be able to look back over how far we have journeyed and be amazed.

Right now, we are in the lowlands, but it is not where we are meant to stay. Join me in taking five big steps to the top. We will go though denial, anger, sadness, and bargaining and finally summit on the mount of acceptance. We have a map to lead us from point to point and bring us to our desired destination and we have a Great Guide. Right now, we are at rock bottom and the only way to go is up.

Stages of Grief

Grief has been defined, by much more learned people than me, as having five stages. The stages are denial, anger, sadness, bargaining, and finally, acceptance. Most of us are aware of these phases of grief. What I don't think we are aware of, or have much coaching on, is how to navigate through these stages. We all want to get through these five stages as quickly as possible, and as fully as we need to, for healing. But how do we grieve gracefully?

Antidotes for Grief

In this book you are given five antidotes for grieving: one antidote for each of the five stages of grief. Antidotes are a form of medicine administered to neutralize the negative effects of some condition. Antidotes hold in themselves the exact properties needed to counteract the existing condition. This medicine allows the body to return to health and wholeness.

It is my belief that the knowledge and application of these grief antidotes can vastly improve the healing process. I don't profess that you will be able to avoid the grief process altogether; that is impossible. What I do think is possible is to be able to grieve gracefully. You can maneuver through grief with some knowledge of what each stage might look like, and at the same time, feel equipped with the antidotes necessary to counteract each stage of grief. These medications for the grieving heart can help you reach the desired outcome: healing.

Keys to Unlock Grief

Maybe you can visualize the analogy of keys and doors better than antidotes. It is the same process, just a different way of describing it. Picture the five stages of grief as five doors. At each stage of grieving, you will be gifted with a key.

21

There is no master key. Each stage has its own specific key that will only unlock the door that you are facing.

Each door you unlock will lead you to another, until you pass through all five doors and reach the end of this hallway we call grief. There are five doors and there are five keys. Are you ready to unlock the grip of grief?

Relax as much as possible, and open your mind to the possibility of grieving gracefully. If at any point you find yourself fumbling with the key, just breathe and remind yourself that this is a process and give yourself grace. After all, grace is the most important element needed at any stage of life.

DREAM is an acronym for the 5 keys to unlock the grip of grief. Here are the 5 keys. Grab your keys and let's get started. Let's DREAM.

D=Dare to Dream
R=Remove the Stinger
E=Embrace Awkward
A=Ask for Help
M=Move On

A Prayer for DREAMers

Great God, You are birthing something holy through this DREAM book. My prayer is that DREAM will… Speak Life, Cultivate Courage, Spark Laughter, and Awaken Dreams. I trust Your Spirit to translate my words into Your words. Illuminate this book with Your eternal light. May it bring deep soul healing. Anoint these writings to free minds, unlock grief, and release those who have been stuck in grief into newness of life.

Penetrate our pain, Lord. Dismantle Denial. Disarm Anger. Satiate Sadness. Quiet our Bargaining...and Lock in Acceptance.

Lord, whether we are grieving from a loss or we are grieving from an unfulfilled longing, we need You. Bind up our brokenness and free us from our sorrow.

Chapter 1

Dare to Dream: Unlock Denial

We will start out right where you landed when circumstances brought you into this valley. When grief enters, denial comes with it. Denial is a gift to your heart to soften the blow. This early phase of grief allows you to perform normal tasks while grieving; routine, daily things like brushing your teeth and dressing yourself. If it weren't for denial, you would not be able to function at all.

Denial is a mental fog, an emotional tranquilizer, and a suppressant to your nerves. Without denial, you would have a nervous breakdown. In denial, reality is softened for a season so that you can wade into the full truth of what you have just experienced and not be swept away with the tide. Denial is meant to be a natural pain suppressant as you adjust to the facts surrounding a loss or longing. Your body would overload and shut down, so God instituted denial as a gift. Receive it as a gift. Be thankful for the time and space denial affords you to adjust to the heartache.

Denial allows you to slowly absorb the pain as you can handle it. In the case of death, it grants you the ability to pick out a casket, plan a memorial, or walk past the empty bedroom and not shut down completely. It is the God-given haze that enables you to go to a viewing or stand in a long receiving line and not collapse. Denial is a coping mechanism that props you up, so you won't fall over.

Softened Reality

The truth will eventually be fully revealed, but for now denial allows the picture to develop slowly. This gives your mind, body, and spirit time to take it in without being overcome. Denial helps you to function when you would be paralyzed without it. Granted, you may function in a much slower mode, but you will be able to function nonetheless. Denial does not totally eliminate the pain. You are aware on some level of the severity of the situation, but it's toned down. Denial is like a dimmer on a light switch that adjusts down from full light to medium to soft. Softer. Not as harsh. Denial allows you the fortitude to pay bills and put gas in your car and remember to close the garage door when you would otherwise lie in a heap on the floor.

Shock

Denial is sometimes called shock, which is very descriptive to me. The news can send shock waves right though us. It makes sense that the griever would go into shock. When you are severely injured, the body goes into shock mode. Automatic reserves of energy are channeled to critical life-sustaining organs. Non-essential functions are put on hold to empower the body to perform life-saving measures.

In denial, survival is paramount, so other peripheral tasks are dismissed until the person can be stabilized.

Denial Descends

Denial is a gift. Denial can come on quickly as was the case for me – my husband died unexpectedly. Denial can also descend slowly – a prolonged marriage issue that leads to filing for separation, fighting over custody of the children, and finally, the divorce decree. Denial can descend slowly as in the case of decreased health. Diagnostic tests are run, lifestyle changes are implemented, and denial seems to accumulate over time.

Denial is harder to identify when it's associated with longing. Let me give an example. I long to be married again. The problem is I have not found the one my heart loves. In the meantime, my radar is up for this man. Because I want to find him so badly, I can overlook obvious red flags. This man in the band is not meant to be my soul mate. He is only 30. I am 50. But denial is sneaky. It's important for us to be aware of the reality altering effects of denial, whether it comes on quickly or descends on us slowly over time.

God Has Got You

When Mike was dying in the driveway on that Tuesday (already dead, we just didn't know it yet) God spoke to me. It was not out loud, but I heard it just the same. While the paramedics were

27

working on Mike, trying to get his heart to start again, we started to pray. The girls and I and two dear neighbor ladies huddled together at the other end of the driveway. I needed God to hear me and I needed to hear from Him. We prayed for Mike and the paramedics and then I paused. Everything started moving in slow motion – it was so surreal. I threw my head back and looked toward heaven. As I looked into the dark night sky, I felt a safety net descending from heaven and over us all. God said, "I've got you...I've got the girls. I have Mike. I've got you. I've got you."

Denial descended like a warm blanket over us to soften the severity of the situation.

I knew by the way God said it that Mike was not coming back. God was assuring me that He had Mike with Him, but also He was also reassuring me that the girls and I were in His tender care. God got us through that night when the doctor came and told us Mike was dead, and God has gotten us through every day since then. God has got me. God has my girls. And God has Mike. In life, and in death, we are safe with God. His arms are big enough to hold up the living and the dying at the same time. His hands are big enough to hold whatever pain you are going through, whatever crisis, whatever diagnosis, whatever layoff, whatever heartbreak or whatever battle it is that you are facing today. God has the power to sustain you through circumstances which would otherwise overwhelm you.

Do you hear God telling you that He has got you? Can you hear Him reminding you that He will get you through this? I hope you hear these whispers from heaven to your heart: "I've got you." God is with you now and He will get you through this.

Spirit

My new "highest learning" is to ask for more of the Spirit. I used to ask God for strength to help me to love even when my heart was broken and have patience even while I was hurting. I asked for certain things to be in my life. I needed the fruits of the Spirit: love, joy, peace, patience, kindness, goodness, faithfulness, gentleness, and self-control. I needed these virtues in my heart. Well, even after years of praying for these things, I continued to struggle. I never felt like my prayers worked very well. Instead of feeling free and flowing, they felt pushed and contrived.

Then recently, I realized that I don't need to keep asking for the gifts of the Spirit (i.e., love, joy, peace, patience). I just need to ask for more SPIRIT! With the Spirit come the gifts. I was trying to get the gifts without the giver. Now I am praying for more Spirit. The Spirit then, naturally and organically, produces these gifts in my life. It is hard to explain, but it was like I was trying to produce milk without having the cow! Hard to do! So now I just ask for the Spirit and I get the gifts automatically. I feel like for years I was doing it backwards and feeling frustrated. It feels much better now.

Spirit is what gives us the ability to grieve gracefully. We will need love, joy, peace, patience, kindness, goodness, faithfulness, gentleness and self-control like never before in our lives. In order to make it through to healing, we will need the gifts of the Spirit. But more importantly, we will need the Spirit.

29

God Is With Us

When I said that God was with us in the driveway, I meant the Spirit of God was with us. If you have never invited the Spirit of God into your life, now is the time. Ask God to be with you. Ask for His Spirit to guide, comfort, and sustain you. God's Spirit can bring you supernatural gifts and you will need them. If you already have the Spirit inside you, pray for increased awareness of this supernatural Comforter. You will need it; grieving is hard work. Ask for God's Spirit to be with you as you grieve.

Maybe you don't feel like you can DREAM. The only way to DREAM at this stage is through the power of God's Spirit living in our grieving souls. If you want victory, you will need the Victor living in your heart. Pray and think about this. It will make all the difference in the world.

Time Heals All Wounds?

They say that time heals all wounds, but I don't believe that time has any real power to heal unless it is combined with other healing agents. I have met people who are stuck in time. They are no more healed now than when loss visited or death struck. Trapped in grief and unable to move forward, they are stuck in the past. Time has gone on, but healing has not happened. It's more like perpetual pain.

If you are several months into grieving and you don't have any emotions welling up in you yet, that means that you are still in shock and denial. You may have decided to camp out in denial. Well, maybe not consciously, but subconsciously. Remember that in order to get to acceptance, which is the goal of grieving, you will need to take five steps.

Parking on Denial Island will not bring you peace, but you might not know how to leave it. The step that allows you to leave denial and enter the next phase of grieving on your way to healing is a daring move. It's a leap of faith, you might say. In this chapter, we will take a closer look at what it takes to move on from denial and step into reality.

Time does not heal on it's own. Time only brings healing when combined with intentional grieving. Otherwise, time is useless and only ticks away the hours and days. Time, by itself does not reduce the pain, heal the brokenness, or lead to transformation. In fact, I believe without healing, time can be cruel.

In The Meantime

Time moves slowly when you are grieving. The days seem to drag on and the hours seem arduous. Empty arms and hollow space weigh heavy on our hearts. The hardest part about grieving is that there is not much we can do to make the grieving go faster. It takes its own sweet time, only the time is not sweet. It is mean. I call it "the meantime." The meantime is when you wish the grieving were over, but it's not. Grief feels like a bully that just won't leave you alone.

I hold onto the scriptures that remind me God has plans for me, but when will I get to see the plans? I know that God has plans to prosper me and not to harm me, to give me hope and a

31

future. But I need hope now. I need to feel God in the present. I know He has future plans for me, but what about now? Right now? What about "in the meantime"? I am ready to move out of this meantime. Let's get on with the grieving, so we can get to the healing. Instead of time feeling mean, I want my time to be meaningful. I'm ready. I think. Lord, make me ready.

Three Grievers

In my conversations with people who have experienced a loss - whether death, divorce, job loss, infertility, or other loss - there seem to be three main categories of grievers. There are those who fight it, those who run from it, and those who make peace with it. I have simplified the terms I will use to define these groups of grievers into Fighters, Flighters, and Get-it-Righters. Let's explore what I mean by each of these.

Fighters

First of all, Fighters are the individuals who are completely overwhelmed by the thought of grieving and so they fight it. They stand opposed to the whole grieving process, and struggle against it. Fighters are not necessarily aggressive people in general, but when faced with difficult emotions, they fight. They fight back the tears, they kick their feelings into the back room, and they scratch their way through anger.

Most Fighters are silent on the outside, but screaming on the inside.

They feel like their emotions are attacking them and so they fight back. Grief feels like a bully threatening their survival, so grief becomes the enemy. Battle lines are drawn out and a full out war begins. They fight against their own emotions, which leads to more pain, frustration, and isolation.

Fighters do not want to wage war; they just feel backed into a corner. Their survival instinct kicks in, and they come out kicking. The tragedy of it all is that Fighters end up hurting themselves even more and alienating those around them. Fighters are not so easy to live with. They walk around in defensive mode and have an uneasy edge to them. Fighters are well-meaning people who just get scared. They are scared to death and feel like their very life is on the line, not so much physically, but emotionally. Fighters fight their feelings so that they can avoid the pain, when in reality they end up fighting the healing.

Flighters

Our second group of grievers is Flighters. Flighters do everything they can to avoid the grieving process. They run from their feelings. Whenever anger or sadness or sorrow comes up in their heart, they turn quickly away from those feelings. Most often these Flighters do so because they feel unable to deal with the emotions. Overwhelmed by their loss, their temporary solution is to detour around the "accident." They head away from their grief, which is the opposite direction of healing.

33

Flighters will run to avoid grief. They run from their pain to work, to activities, to relationships, to coping mechanisms, to volunteer work, and to distractions - constructive or destructive.

None of these things would throw their life into chaos, but done in excess, done in avoidance, done in distraction, the pain is compounded.

Now, I don't believe that Flighters are consciously aware that they are averting the grieving process. If they are aware of this deliberate distraction, they have every intention of circling back to do the grieving later. Maybe when they are stronger or when a little more time has passed by, and it doesn't seem so fresh or so raw to manage.

The problem is that for Flighters, there never seems to be an appropriate time for them to grieve. There is always something else that draws their attention. They never seem to detour back and find the healing they so desperately need. Each time they think about approaching the grieving process, they feel the need to run.

In contrast to Fighters, Flighters don't actively push away the grief - they just avoid it. They divert their attention to matters that seem less threatening and much easier to manage. Flight is a natural response and doesn't present an initial problem for the Flighters. But if they continue to navigate away from their feelings, healing is delayed.

Flighters would much rather do anything than face their hard-to-deal-with emotions like anger, sadness, and loneliness. Frankly, none of us likes to grieve, but Flighters seem to be paralyzed by these emotions. Grief, for them, is like jail and their grieving emotions like ugly cell mates. The

34

last thing they would want to do is to be locked up with their emotions.

Fight and flight are instinctual responses to threatening situations, people, or feelings. We perceive grief as threatening to us. Although fight and flight are natural at the beginning of grief, we want to graduate to the third category of grieving – get-it-right.

Get-It-Righters

Get-It-Righters are what we all want to eventually become so that we can be healed. When it comes to grief and grieving, we all want to "get it right." So whether we start out as Fighters or Flighters our goal is to end up as Get-It-Righters. A Get-it-Righter is a Fighter or a Flighter who has just learned how to deal with emotions differently. Instead of continuing to Fight or Flight, they learn how to grieve until the hurt is absorbed and healing happens.

I gave catchy titles to these categories of grievers so that we can identify ourselves in the process and adjust our approach as we go. We can recognize when we are fighting our emotional healing or when we are attempting to take flight from challenging feelings. Maybe we even say out loud to ourselves, "I am fighting with myself" or "I am taking flight to avoid dealing with some hard emotions." Once we are able to accurately identify when we are caught up in one of these natural responses to fear, we can stop and redirect. Stop the fighting or cease the flighting and then tap into our supernatural ability to heal.

Fight and flight are natural instincts and they serve the purpose of helping us to avoid threats. They are God-given reactions to keep us safe in the face of danger. But at some point, we want to tap into our other God-given abilities so that we can go beyond mere survival, and on to thriving.

You can easily determine if you are stuck in survival mode if you are still fighting or flighting. My goal is to help you and me move into healing, so that we can go on to live and thrive. So, how do we do that? How do we live with grief and loss and incorporate them into our everyday lives? How do we face the once threatening fear and not fight or flight?

Key to Unlock Denial:
Dare To Dream

Basically, if you are a griever in denial, something traumatic has happened to you. In my case, someone I love died. I would say it this way: you are waking up to the nightmare. As denial fades, you could be saying to yourself, "This is a nightmare!" The love of your life found another love. Your child dies as a result of a rare brain disorder. Or you slowly watched your mom fade away into someone unfamiliar. These are our worst nightmares! Only, for you, these aren't visions you have in your sleep, these are your reality. No one wants to wake up from nightmares like these and realize they are real. There is only one solution: when the nightmare happens, you have to Dare to Dream.

Let me explain what I mean by Dare to Dream. When you begin to wake up and realize this nightmare is for real, you must Dare to Dream of what life could look like after the nightmare is over.

Daring to Dream lets your spirit look past the nightmare and into the proposed future, so you can see yourself surviving. Unless we can see ourselves making it through a scary phase, we will not even enter into it. Grief is sent to help us through the valley of the shadow of death, out of the pit of loss, and over the hot coals of longing.

Daring to Dream is the antidote to the nightmare you are in. It is the leap of faith that propels you out of the nightmare and into the healing process. I know this may sound like too big of a leap, but it is only a step. Don't dismiss this dare until you give it a try.

Dare to Dream and just allow your mind to entertain the idea that you could survive this. Picture that - one day - in the not-too-distant future, you may actually smile again. Visualize yourself adjusting and finding balance and able to take full breaths. Imagine your home environment not so stressed and eventually becoming peaceful. This will stretch you, but try to see yourself happy. Hard to do, isn't it? It is hard to imagine that you will ever wake up without the horrible feeling in the pit of your stomach, sleep through the night, or have energy and excitement for the coming workweek, but you need to believe it, even if you can't see it yet.

Dream in Color

You have to neutralize the nightmare by introducing little shots of dreams. Dare to Dream of restored relationships, renewed joy, and rejuvenated stamina. Dream in color against the black and white backdrop of your grieving existence. See splashes of bright paints infusing your life canvas with large, lush brush strokes.

The nightmare happened against your will. You would never have wished this into existence. Where the nightmare came on you with no choice, the dream will only come if invited. Nightmares depress us. Dreams lift us up. Will you chose to stay stuck in the nightmare or Dare to Dream?

Try it: Dare to Dream. Believe that you will make it through this and you will take the first step toward wholeness. Hold onto hope. Hope is necessary for dreaming.

Hope Defined

What is hope? Hope might be easier to define by what it is NOT. Hope is not wishing—wishing still leaves you hopeless. Wishing is like a distant, far away longing that only has a slight possibility of coming true. Wishing still leaves you vulnerable and afraid and stranded.

Hope, on the other hand, is truth that transcends your current circumstances. Hope is the solid belief that propels you forward with certainty of a positive outcome. Hope believes that you will make it through, that you will grow from this, and that you will come out on the other side a transformed person.

Hope is being absolutely certain that there is nothing you can go through that will take your spirit down.

Hope is what gets you up in the mornings. It's what gets you through the days. And it's what gets you through the long nights. Hope is the powerful ingredient that makes everything doable. Without it, we are doomed. With hope, we are indestructible. Hope is what gives your heart lift.

Hope does not take grief away, but it provides a safe passage through the tunnel of grief. Hope shines light into the dark passage, so that you can find your way. Hope beckons you forward. Hope is the way out and the way through. Without hope, we would soon drop into despair and darkness. Hope is the ray of light that dispels the darkness and illuminates the path. Hope IS the way.

Where can you get hope?

The frustrating thing about hope is that it cannot be manufactured. Hope is not a product you can put on your shopping list and pick up at the store on your way home from work. It cannot be purchased on the internet. In fact, it cannot be bought at all. So how do we get hope?

Free Gift

Hope is a free gift. Hope is yours for the asking. Hope will cost you nothing and give you everything. Where can you get this free gift, with no purchase necessary? There is only one place: it lives in the heart. Your heart. My heart. All humans have hope in their hearts. Our Creator deposited hope into our hearts when He made us. He knew that our hearts would break and He also knew that the only thing to heal a broken heart would be hope. So God put hope right where it would be needed.

Peer into a human heart and you will find the home of hope. It is usually when our hearts are broken that we find hope. There's something about our hearts breaking open that allows hope to come out. Some people spend their whole lives trying to keep their hearts from being broken; they don't want to be hurt. But it has been my experience that when my heart has been broken - broken by people or broken for people - my heart actually heals. Compassion expands my heart and, with hope at the center of it, healing happens.

You can spend your whole life keeping people at an arm's distance so that no one gets close enough to touch your heart for fear of it breaking. That is a seemingly safe, but lonely, existence. Or, you can choose to love and risk emotional security knowing if your heart does break, it can heal.

Broken Hearts Can Heal

Notice I said the heart CAN heal. Daring to Dream does not automatically heal a broken heart. As a young widow, I hear lots of stories of broken hearts. I will be honest with you, not all broken hearts heal. I have met some people who have had severe losses and yet they hold onto hope. Their hearts are healing and hopeful. But the greater numbers of people I encounter do not have healing.

They simply do not know how to fix their broken hearts. Until you have had your heart broken by death, divorce, or disappointment, you probably don't know what you would do. But once they enter, it is my hope that you can know what to do to have healing. Hope and healing are intermingled and somewhat inseparable. You can't have healing without hope, and hope automatically leads to healing.

Healing in the Heart

When I pray for hope and healing for someone who's child has died or spouse passed away or lost their mother to a terminal disease, I am not praying for them to have their loved ones back physically. Death is a one-way door that leads to the other side and there is no way back through that turnstile. There is no possible way to physically bring someone back to this life once they have officially passed over. We can't bring the dead back to life here on Earth.

Our hope cannot be based on physical healing.

When my husband died, I wished that I could see him and kiss him one more time. I wished that my girls could have their dad walk them down the aisle at their future weddings. I wished that Mike's family could hug him at the holidays and that his friends could still meet him for lunch. Wishing things were different could not bring one ounce of healing to any of us. We needed hope to heal our hearts.

41

Engaged

When my daughter Abbi got engaged one year after her dad's death, the most frequently asked question I heard was, "Who is going to walk Abbi down the aisle?" During all the wedding preparations, Abbi contemplated alternative companions for that journey. She thought about having one of her uncles take her dad's place. Then she thought of asking one of her close male friends, her grandpa, her fiancé's dad, or even me to escort her toward the altar. These were all quality options, but Abbi came to the realization that there was indeed no one who could take her dad's place. She decided to walk by herself in the strength and love that her father had given her. She chose to Dare to Dream.

This was a brave move. Walking that runway alone, without her dad, would take courage, and Abbi prepared well for it. By the wedding day, her heart was strong.

Yes, she physically missed her dad being able to delight in her as a bride and escorting her to her beloved, but Abbi was not limited by the physical separation of death.

Down the Aisle

When the big day came, it was magnificent! Her sister and bridesmaids had cleared the way for her down the aisle. Her husband-to-be stepped forward ready to receive his glorious bride at the altar. The whole room filled with anxious anticipation. There was a powerful transition in the music and as it swelled, so did the tears.

We all watched the back of the room waiting for the bride to appear. At the climax of the music two doors swung wide open and there she stood, regal and ready. We all rose to our feet out of respect for what was transpiring and there was an audible gasp as she stepped forward.

Abbi owned the moment. She walked the runway with grace and beauty and poise becoming of a young woman who was so dearly loved by her dad. Mike was not there physically, but he was there. Her dad was not there holding her arm, but he was there holding her heart. She shined like the radiant daughter that she was and the wife she was about to become. There was not a hint of sorrow in that moment. Did Abbi miss her dad? Yes, and always will. But hope shines brightly and the church was flooded with light that day. Hope is holy. Hope is sacred. Hope is powerful.

The healing that Abbi had allowed in her heart helped us all heal a little more that day.

Hope is Contagious

When one person chooses to Dare to Dream and walk in the strength and humility of hope, we are all given the opportunity to heal. Hope is powerful. It can deliver a young bride to her groom and it can fill a room. Hope happens when a single soul chooses to believe, chooses to heal, and chooses to see beyond the pain to the other side. It's seen in the small, everyday moments and the pivotal, profound transitions.

Hope stands in the face of fear and melts it away. Hope dissolves distrust and discouragement. Hope overpowers grief and delivers courage

43

to the defeated and lets healing begin. Hope bridges the gap between loss and longing, and leads us safely across the river of uncertainty. Hope is vital, necessary, and essential. Without it, we are surely doomed. With hope, we are securely delivered.

It is my sincere prayer that you have hope.

Seasons

Although hope is contagious, it is not completely transferable. You have to Dare to Dream and find hope in your own heart for it to work. You can be affected by another person's hope, but it cannot heal you unless it is your own.

In early fall, about one year after my husband's death, I came across an email invite to a spiritual retreat hosted by Nicole Johnson. Nicole is a beloved author and an amazing dramatic presenter, and I had always loved her work. Her dramas from the "Women of Faith" conferences had impacted me so profoundly that even years later, I could recall with clarity several of her one-woman acts. I had seen her box with cancer, boat with grief, and backpack with brokenness. Nicole has a gift for bringing real life situations to light through humor and acting. She dives into the heart of our pain to provide emotional healing and spiritual learning. I knew that Nicole was a trustworthy source of truth and grace.

The email invitation said that Nicole was hosting a new style of spiritual retreat called "Seasons," and it was coming to my area of the country later that fall. I signed up instantly.

The retreat turned out to be even more amazing than I had ever imagined.

Nicole was authentic and engaging, the music was magical, and the speakers were open and vulnerable about their struggles and their triumphs. The weekend was tangible healing for my heart and soul.

Hope Heals

One of the most inspiring sessions at the retreat actually came from a young married couple named Jay and Katherine Wolf. They had started a ministry called "Hope Heals."

This lawyer and former model had moved to California to live the dream. They soon had a beautiful baby boy and life was indeed good. You might even say picture-perfect. They loved each other, their new bundle of joy, and God. They knew God loved them and had big plans for them. They just didn't know what those plans would turn out to be.

One day their picture-perfect life came crashing to the floor when Katherine collapsed in their small California apartment. Katherine had put their six-month-old baby down for a nap. By the grace of God, Jay had just come home to work on a paper for his law degree. Jay was in the other room when he heard his wife fall and was able to get medical help right away. What they didn't know then, but soon found out, was that Katherine had suffered a major stroke and would be partially paralyzed for the rest of her life. Their picture-perfect life was gone forever.

Jay and Katherine shared their story with us at this retreat. Katherine had endured years of intensive care, hospital stays, surgeries, rehab, and ongoing therapy. She learned to live life daily with physical difficulties and limitations. Jay has had to watch his wife suffer, and he suffers along with her. Jay was a picture of a groom loving his broken bride in a Jesus-like way. It would be easy to feel sorry for them after all that happened. To see them sharing their personal story, loving each other, and delivering their message of "Hope Heals," I was inspired by their passion. Even though they had been broken, they had hope, and hope heals.

Katherine's spirit burst forth with laughter and life and a joy that astounded me. Jay spoke gently and directly about how God carried them through this horrible trial. They both reflect the image of true healing: hope has healed them. Katherine's indomitable spirit and Jay's unfailing love and devotion shine.

I will never forget Katherine telling us, "This is my joy. You can't have it!" And she was right. Although her joy was contagious, it was not altogether transferrable. She was telling us to tap into our own hearts and find our own joy in God. That is where true joy is found, and where healing abounds. We can't steal someone else's joy - we have to get our own from God. Jay and Katherine were timely examples to me of two souls doing the hard work of grieving for what had been lost in their lives, but also celebrating those qualities that can never be taken away. Faith, hope, and love become more precious in the face of disaster and recovery.

Your Season

If you are reading this book, you need hope. Whatever season of distress you have entered, hope is what you need more than anything else. I hope you will be encouraged by my friends, Jay and Katherine, and my daughter, Abbi, to find joy and hope for your heart. God longs to love you and give you hope that heals. Your heart needs wings to lift you above the circumstances of your season and into the certainty of God's unchanging devotion to you.

Don't linger in the meantime. Be diligent at doing the real work of grieving. You don't want to be stuck in the winter of your soul. Seasons change. Claim spring in your heart and Dare to Dream knowing that God will bring you through grief and into grace. Hold onto hope. God is holding onto you.

Dare to Dream. I say "Dare" because at some point, denial becomes a choice. When denial becomes comfortable, we have to choose to break out of it. It takes concerted effort to Dare to Dream. For me, dreaming and dancing go together. When denial gets taken too far, you might need to bust out of it. Let's see if you can bust out some dance moves.

Dare to Dance

Let me give you some help with this, because I know it is hard. Sometimes Daring to Dream might require learning some new dance moves.

I have been wrestling with a persistent thought lately, which is this: what if, when I approach a roadblock in my life, I would decide to dance instead of despair? When I find myself backed into a corner or at a dead end, what if I would choose to celebrate and believe beyond my circumstances? When I can't see my way out, what if I put my trust in God instead of chronically questioning His ability to get me through? How would this change my life? If I were able to put my trust in God and celebrate before I see the deliverance, how would this simple act of obedience change my day-to-day life?

You see, it has struck me that it is natural to applaud after the victory game. It takes no faith to thank God when he has led me through some trial. It is a mere act of gratitude, like when you send someone a thank you note for a gift they gave you. That's polite. Good manners.

But I am being challenged by a higher thought than thank you notes. The challenge I am hearing is this…What if I would dare to dance before the deliverance? What if I would, with full trust and faith in God, go ahead and do a little dance at the dead end, knowing that God will get me through whatever obstacles I face in this life? How would it look to integrate this one philosophy into my routine?

Dead-end Dances

This is the challenge that called my name. I recently completed a Bible study called "Lord, Change My Attitude" by James MacDonald. He was teaching on the passage where the children of Israel were being freed from hundreds of years of slavery.

It's such a dramatic story with Moses as the lead character up against the Egyptian ruler. It's a showdown between God and Pharaoh. There are plaques and pestilence and problems all along this road to freedom.

Note: The road to freedom is often a bumpy ride.

James MacDonald points out that when the children of Israel (which were actually adults and children—God just called them all His children, regardless of age) got to each roadblock, they would cry out for God to save them! Miraculously God provided a cloud by day to lead them and a fire by night to be their night light (evidently they were afraid of the dark).

In the climax of the story, these slaves come to a freedom road dead-end, a trap. They are up against a wall. Actually, it isn't a wall, it's water – The Red Sea. There seems to be no way out of this! But never fear—God shows up and saves them again. He makes a porthole through to the other side. Literally, they are able to pass through impassible waters. God safely delivers them through this deadly dead-end situation without one casualty of these now freed people. God kills all the bad guys in the same spot where he gives His children a new lease on life.

Victory Dance

When the children of Israel made it through, when they all got to the other side of this seemingly "no way out alive" situation, they celebrated. They sang and danced and Moses' sister led them all in a flash-mob dance of victory. It was a lively ending to a dead-end scene.

Okay, back to me sitting there watching James MacDonald on the video teaching about attitudes, when all of the sudden this action-packed story from ancient times is speaking to me personally. Here is what I heard James say: how great would it have been if they had believed God and danced on the Egyptian side of the Red Sea?

What if these children had dared to dance, before the deliverance?

What if the people would have celebrated in assurance of their safe passage?

This is what I call DARE TO DANCE. WOW! I need to dare to dance!

Pre-Game Dance

Now you see why this thought has been messing with my mind. It is one thing to thank God after He gets you through the awful, the unthinkable, and the tragic. But I think God wants me to DARE TO DANCE before he brings me safely to the other side. God deserves our dance because He is faithful to deliver us. Dance for the Deliverer before you are delivered. This one act of faith will catapult your heart on the other side of the tragedy. From this side of the awful, you can send your heart to the other side—to the delivered side—by choosing to dance. If you and I claim victory by the power of the Almighty to help us overcome whatever it is we face, then we will be DARING TO DANCE! And the devil hates when we do this kind of dance because he knows he is already defeated.

Time to Dance

I think that I need to do some "dancing on the devil!" How about you? Some Satan-stomping! Are you with me? Do you feel the beat? Can you hear the music of your heart? Your soul song? And I think it is time to go dancing. This may sound too girly for you real men out there. Okay, men, do a victory dance before the big game and see if that will change how you play the game, your attitude toward the other players, or the atmosphere in the locker room. Then approach the playing field humbly, knowing that God is your strength. God is your victory maker. And then enjoy the game! Dare to dance.

Prayer for Dare to Dream

Dear Lord, grant us the ability to see the blessings we have around us, even as we grieve what we do not have. All is not lost. Give us eyes to see what remains and give us thankful hearts for the remnant of life that endures. Help us to see beyond our own grief. Enable our hearts to dream and dance. Keep us from getting lost in the grief. Remind us to live out our days with purpose. Empower us to see your love and bind our broken hearts to You.

May death's power be restrained so that those who continue to live can find greater meaning to their lives, and may relationship bonds only increase. Whether we are grieving from the loss of something we once had, or we are grieving from the longing for something we do not have yet, help us grieve gracefully. Give us abundant grace

51

for our hearts to heal. Preserve our hearts in Your unending love and give us peace that can only come from You.

God, we are utterly dependent on You to console our sorrow and reclaim our hope.

Through Jesus, who conquered all, we ask all these things. Amen.

Chapter 2

Remove the Stinger:

Unlock Anger

The second stage of grief for me was anger and this is something I felt intensely. I was mad that my love was taken from me. I was angry because he was not old enough to die. I was enraged that I had to leave the hospital and go home without him. I was furious he would never come home again. It is perfectly normal to be mad. I won't try to talk you out of it; my goal is to talk you through it. Whether you are mad because you have lost something or because you long to have something, your anger will look similar.

You will know that denial is fading when you find yourself getting mad. To move from denial to anger is a step up? Yes! If you find yourself mad at the cat, cussing in traffic (more than you usually do), and needing to vent some built up frustrations, this is a good thing. It means your body is allowing the full reality of what you experienced to be felt.

You will be angry, and that will lead you in the right direction for healing.

This phase of grief will seem obvious to you when you enter it. You will be mad at the loss or angry at the thought of living without what you long for. I was frustrated that my husband had died and we did not even make it to our 25th wedding anniversary. I was upset that the girls would not have their father to love them the rest of their lives. I was angry that I had to sleep alone at night, mad that I had to learn how to parent the girls on my own, and upset that I had to go to church and sit there without my spiritual partner. I was miffed that I had to go to family functions without my husband. His birthday and our anniversary were hard days, and I felt angry that they were stolen from me.

So you might be angry at the specific loss or longing, but you might also just be mad at everything related to it. There were so many maddening things that I had no choice in that came along with the death. They were thrust upon me and I just had to learn how to manage. This made me even madder. Not only was I grieving the separation and abandonment that death imposed, I was also dealing with so many everyday tasks that this change demanded. Tasks like changing every single document with his name on it. Insurance, house, cars, bank accounts, and bills all had to be changed to my name. His name erased off of the accounts. It made me mad for the workload of changing all the details, but I was also mad that we were deleting him from my life.

I did not want to delete his name, but it was necessary because he was gone.

In the case of longing, you may be mad that you got another invitation to a baby shower and you still long for a child. You may be bothered to be asked to be a bridesmaid and yet what you want is to be a bride. Maybe you work with a guy who doesn't treat women with respect, but somehow he always has a date. You can't remember the last date you had.

Grief as an Intruder

Grief: I hated that word and every place that it had invaded in our lives. Grief was not an invited guest in our house, but an intruder. Grief had taken my husband and stolen my future with him. How cruel! How brutal! How dare grief do this to the girls and me! But grief does not respect people. Grief is rude and unruly. Grief goes where it pleases, takes whomever it wants, and there is nothing we can do about it. Grief deals its menace and we are unwilling recipients of its fallout.

The helplessness to undo what had been done to us made me so mad. Grief had the upper hand, and I was losing. Grief made me do things I did not want to do; things like staring at my dead husband's clothes hanging in what used to be our closet. I could have the whole closet to myself now, but I didn't want closet space - I wanted my husband. Grief deals, and we reel.

In the anger stage of grief, you will be mad at the unwanted changes inflicted upon you or mad that changes you long for have not happened. You will find this all hard to accept. You will most likely be frustrated that you have to learn how to go on without what you want, maybe even enraged that you have to do this. You don't want to play with this lousy hand you have been dealt, but you have no choice. This IS your hand.

Healthy Anger

As denial recedes and anger enters your grief, know that you are right on track with healing. Getting mad is part of what it takes to get better. But a word of caution here: it is important for you to recognize that you are angry at things you can't change. So get mad! Vent and yell and journal and punch your pillow and stomp your feet. Release your anger, but don't hurt yourself or others. Be angry, and sin not.

- Write "hate mail," but don't send it.
- Vent to safe friends who you know you can trust.
- Journal about the anger and frustration and madness.
- Find healthy outlets for your anger like yoga.
- Get some fresh air.
- Go for a walk or work out at the gym.
- Put on your boxing gloves and wail on the punching bag.

Madness will flare and recede in this stage, but the overall feeling will be intense anger. I want to validate your anger.

Seeing your ex-husband move his new girlfriend into "your" house will make anyone angry. When the promotion that you have been working so hard for goes to someone outside the company, it's reasonable to get mad. But if you find yourself unable to process your anger and feel stuck in the madness, take a closer look at what you are mad about and ask for God's help to heal.

Key to Unlock Anger:
Remove the Stinger

Do you remember the first time you were stung by a bee as a kid? I do. It hurt! I shouted and jumped back and was so mad at that little winged thing that stung me! So I killed it. I smashed it. Then I went to get some love, because love always helps when we are hurt. Mom would look at the sting spot and kiss it, because kisses kill bacteria and all forms of illnesses. Hugs and kisses are real medicine. Next she would put a Band-Aid on it. And something about Band-Aids made this bearable—it was almost as if that pink plastic tape would seal in the hugs and kisses and lock in the goodness. Only after the Band-Aid was in place could I wipe my tears and go back to whatever it was I was doing before I got stung.

I remember one time when this nasty bee stung me and left his stinger in my finger. How dare he do that! I was madder than ever! Not only had he stung me, but because he left his stinger in me it felt like I was repeatedly being stung over and over again. I instinctively killed the bee that stung me, but that was not enough to make me feel better. I had to do more. I had to remove the stinger before the pain would stop.

Removing the stinger was tricky, because I had to run and alert mom. Then we had to find the tweezers to finally remove the tiny sliver from my pulsating flesh. It was hard to see the tiny bee-bottom and even harder to grasp with mom's eyebrow tweezers, but at last the extraction brought a sigh of relief. Then there was the usual routine of kisses and hugs and Band-Aids to let the healing begin. Only this time it took a little longer to heal and I also noticed that it took longer for the swelling to go down.

Stingers Keep Stinging

Has this ever happened to you? Have you ever been stung by a bee and not realized the stinger was still in there? Maybe you are playing outside in your bare feet and all of the sudden this shooting pain stops you in your tracks. You've been stung by a bee. You quickly brush the bottom of your foot and get back to playing. Only later when you take a closer look at your foot because it is still bothering you, do you realize that the stinger is still in there. Only by now, the spot is red and swollen and inflamed.

Extraction of the stinger is more painful than the actual bee sting, because it has been left in there to fester and swell and get infected.

Closer Examination

My daughter Faith had a questionable mole removed before the beginning of the school year. The test results came back still borderline for skin cancer, and so we went to a plastic surgeon to have a bigger section of tissue removed. Better to be safe than sorry with skin cancer running in our family. The plastic surgeon removed the next layer of skin to make sure we got all of the area clean and clear.

But after several months the area was still not healing. We went back to the doctor and had them take a closer look at why it was not healing. One of the stitches that was used to sew the tissue on the inside was not being absorbed into the skin like it was supposed to be and it was keeping the wound from healing.

So, the doctor removed the stitch that was sticking out from Faith's leg and said it would heal in a couple of days. And it did. Maybe there is something preventing your grief from healing, something that was supposed to be absorbed in the healing process that is just not healing properly. If this is the case, go for a closer look.

There are doctors and counselors and grief specialists that can help you. With a closer look, a professional will be able to determine what is keeping your grief from healing. There may be some simple steps that will allow the wound to heal. When the doctor removed the stitch from Faith's leg it was able to heal properly and quickly.

God does not want you to hurt forever. He wants you to heal. He wants the grief wound to heal and you to be whole. Do whatever it takes to bring healing to your heart. You are worth it. Life is meant to be lived. Do not allow grief to hold you back from living the life you are meant to live.

The Sting of Anger

This is how it is when you lose someone, but this is also how it is when you long for someone or something. Pain shoots through your whole body alerting you that something has just happened! You shout! Jump back! And try to figure out what is going on. It stings! We can walk around not even aware that the stinger is still in there. Only after more careful examination do we realize that there is a second step needed for our healing. We have to stop and remove the stinger.

Jesus is the ultimate "sting remover" for these deadly stings. He removed the sting by conquering death and rising to new life! Jesus removed the sting of death for Himself and He wants to remove the sting of death from you and me. Just like when you ran to your mom for help as a kid when you were stung by a bee, run to Jesus to remove the sting of death. Jesus is the only one qualified to remove it; we cannot do this on our own.

Jesus conquered death and the grave and He wants to conquer this in your life. Put your trust in Him to have power over what you are experiencing in grief.

Show Jesus where it hurts. Tell Him all about your pain. Ask Him to remove the damage caused by the sting of death. Sit on His lap and cry into His chest. Healing happens here. And then, when you are done crying it out, when He has eased your pain and put His layer of protection over the wound, get back into life.

It would be a double tragedy if my life stopped when my husband died. Unfortunately, I know there are people out there that exist in this perpetual grieving time. As a widow, I realized there was an appropriate time to take off my grieving shawl. There was a time for me to change out of the black veil and somber face. There is a time for everything. Maybe today is your day to start living again after the death. Just like as kids, we went back to playing again after the bee sting. Get back to life. Jesus came to give you life, take it! Jesus rose again to give us victory over death. Claim life!

Today, I put before you two choices: Life and Death. Choose life! Even in the face of death, I choose to live, because Jesus lives in me. I have victory over death, even death of a spouse.

The Stinger

Jesus removed the sting of death by conquering death with new life. He wants to give you new life and if you are honest with yourself, you need it. But Jesus also wants to remove the stinger of death that may still be stinging you. I have met people who have not been able to heal after the death of a loved one. Have you? We've all seen them. Angry, bitter, filled with a searing rage right under their skin. These people have no idea the coldness in their eyes.

Buried Deep Within

What has kept these people from healing? I don't know enough about their lives to answer this question, but I have some ideas of what could keep them locked in anger. Something is still stinging them, and they have not been able to remove the stinger. Some stinger is buried deep within them that is causing this ongoing pain. What is it that troubles them still?

I know for me there were several things that kept stinging me when Mike died. I thought that we would make it to our 25th wedding anniversary. I thought he would be there on my 50th birthday. I thought he would walk Abbi down the aisle. I thought he would teach Faith to drive.

61

These thoughts kept stinging me. I had to remove the stinger. I had to let go of what I thought was going to happen and make peace with what was happening. This is a delicate process. Acceptance comes slowly. Grieving is the process by which we are able to move through anger and into acceptance.

Get Out the Tweezers

If you find that you are still mad and not able to move through this stage of grieving, get out the magnifying glass and the tweezers. There may be something still buried in your grief that is keeping you from healing. If your anger is still red hot and puffy, there may be something that needs to be removed. If you are still boiling every single day and not able to let go of the anger, you need healing.

Maybe you won't accept the death of your loved one and you think that if you let them go, you will lose them forever. Take a closer look at what keeps hurting you. Maybe it is that you are holding onto a mental image that is not allowing you to move on. Letting go is hard, but holding onto something that is gone only keeps you from moving on. It doesn't keep your parents from divorcing, your mother from getting breast cancer, or bring your brother back to life. Anger just keeps you stuck. How do you remove the stinger and get rid of the anger that is controlling your life?

How to Remove the Stinger

You have heard me stress the importance of removing the stinger of anger, but in order to remove the stinger, you have to find it first. How do you find the stinger? Probably, all you know is that you are mad. Really mad! How do you determine what is stinging you? Start where it hurts.

There is definitely going to be an area of infection surrounding the stinger. A hot spot. You will notice a central theme to your most intense anger. Let's call it your thorn in your flesh. The thing you don't like to think about because it makes you so angry. For instance, the fact that he seems to be getting away with his deception. The idea that she gets to spend time with your kids. The thought that you will never make love to your late husband again. Identify your target area of anger.

Then, look for patterns of anger - collections of hurt that express themselves as rage. Start there. If you are having trouble identifying your stinger ask yourselves one question...and answer it. What is it that makes you mad? I am mad because such and such. Great! Now, we are getting somewhere. Let's keep going. And what about such and such makes you mad? Such and such makes me mad because of X and Y. Yes! Keep digging. And what about X and Y makes you mad?

Keep on asking yourself what you are mad about and this will lead you to the stinger. You will have to take some time exploring your anger, but I promise you will reach the root of your rage. It is vital to find the source of your anger so that you can unlock your grief. The key to unlock anger is to Remove the Stinger.

At first, it was hard to sort through my anger in order to find the stinger. I felt like I was looking for a needle in a haystack. But with diligence and practice I was able to diffuse the bomb of anger I had in my belly.

I had to ask myself some hard questions and be vulnerable enough to answer them honestly. Anger usually answers with sarcasm and hostility but you will know you have reached the stinger when your tone softens. You may even cry. I will give you a glimpse into one of my stinger finding adventures. Here's how it went.

What makes me mad? Isn't it obvious?! Because my husband died! Yes. What about him dying makes me so mad? Because he is not here! Yes. What about him not being here makes me so angry? Because I miss him! Yes. What about missing my late husband makes me mad? He was my love. Yes. What about missing his love makes me mad? It was so special. Yes. What about his love was so special? It was real. Yes. What was so real about your love? He saw me. (Tears well up in my eyes and I know I have found the stinger.) He saw me like no one else in my whole life saw me. He saw me at my best and at my worst, yet he still saw me as beautiful. I feel unseen now that he is gone. I feel invisible. People look at me but don't see me. His eyes reflected back the Kristi that I knew I could be and wanted to be. The Kristi he knew I was deep inside. I lost my husband and now I'm afraid I am losing myself. There was a part of me that I only saw when I looked into his eyes. That's why I am so mad.

That is what really stings my heart. Not only did I lose my soul mate when he died, but now I am afraid I am losing me, too.

When we keep asking questions, it allows us to go below the surface level of annoyances into the real frustrations and finally get to the root of our anger.

What is really bothering you?

Anger is exhausting. It's too intense. It is impossible to keep anger burning unless you keep putting fuel on the fire. At some point, I realized that if I quit putting logs on the fire, the fire would eventually die out. Where was all this extra firewood coming from? I realized I was the one keeping the flame going. I was the one who kept stirring the coals and throwing more wood on the fire. Why? Because I needed to validate my pain. I needed for someone to see my anguish. I was sending up smoke signals, but I was also in danger of burning my own house down. Something had to change.

When we remove the stinger of anger, the fire can die down. By identifying the hot spot of your anger, you can quit poking at the fire and let things cool off. When I was able to sort through all my anger and come to the source of what was really bothering me, I instantly began to feel relief. My anger felt heard. I didn't feel the need to keep sending up smoke signals because the message had been heard and honored.

Sometimes, anger is so deep and so infected it takes concerted effort to remove the stinger. In that case, we call in the heavy machinery.

65

For me, it has been a two-step process, kind of like shampooing your hair is a two-step process. Lather, rinse, repeat. For our purposes...Step one: Prayer. Step two: Layer. Prayer, Layer, repeat. So, let's explore these two simple, yet game-changing and life-giving, steps, so that we can "get it right."

Prayer

What do I mean by Prayer? Will you need to buy any special beads or know any traditional chants? Will you be required to memorize prewritten prayers from a sanctioned book? And what if you have never been a real "Talk to God" kind of person? Will you have to speak your prayers out loud or cross over your heart when you are finished praying? Let me answer most of those questions by simply saying this—what I mean when I say Prayer is to just tell God you are hurting and that you need His help. Something as simple as this: "God, I am hurting and I am asking for Your help."

Grieving is excruciating at times and all of us need help dealing with loss and longing. It would seem cruel for God to expect us to know how to recover from this kind of hurt without help from Him. In this life, we will have challenges that we cannot endure without heavenly help, and grief is one of the hardest. It may seem obvious to say that we need assistance to manage the range of difficult emotions that come with grief, but let me go ahead and be the first one to say it..."I need help! I am not going to make it through this without some divine intervention. I need someone to help me! It would be great if God Himself were available for me to talk to about this. Are you there, God? Do you have time for me? Can I talk to you about what is going on in my heart? Do you care? Can you help?"

Jesus died so that we - human beings - could have direct access to God. How do you like this plan? Unlimited calling. Unlimited prayers. Unlimited minutes. Anyone can talk to God. Anytime. Anywhere. So don't be afraid that you are calling God too often, or you might stay on the line too long. He is on speed dial on my prayer line and He is not bothered by requests. God is our original Father. He cares deeply and passionately for us. He wants us to call Him. He will be glad to hear from you.

So, that's it? I just talk to God and tell Him that I am hurting and ask for His help? Yes, that's basically it! Have you ever been in so much physical pain that it was hard to talk? Kidney stones or labor in childbirth come to my mind. The pain is overwhelming and all you want to do is cry or get some major pain-blocking medications. Your main focus is on getting through the next slight move of the kidney stone or the next contraction.

God understands you are in severe pain when you are grieving. You don't have a lot of energy for chitchat. You just want to cry and you want God to do something about the pain...so just cry out to Him. Nothing profound or eloquent required; just open the channel of communication and ask Him to help you. You don't even have to hit the send button. Prayers automatically rise to God.

Layer

Okay, so I pray. I tell God that this really hurts and I want Him to help me...then what? Prayer and then Layer.

Layer refers to the ability God gives you to stay with your anger, neither fighting it nor running from it, but making peace with the anger. The goal is to sit with the anger long enough for it to dissipate. When you are confronted by angry feelings, ask God to help you layer them with comfort. I picture a quilt. A quilt is made up of multiple pieces of fabric stitched together over time. Individual squares are brought together with a layer of softness in between. Grief is like taking all those individual memories and feelings and bringing them together in prayer and adding a layer of softness for comfort.

Just like praying starts out simple, so does layering. Determine to focus on a what is really making you mad so you don't feel overwhelmed the anger. Don't stay very long. These first few practices will be brief and contained. In time, God will help you incorporate all these strong emotions, but for now we will start out small. Grief can feel overwhelming, so give yourself lots of grace.

Example One

Let me give you an example of layering from my own experience. The loss of my husband's presence here with me was like getting the wind knocked out of me. My lungs did not know how to fill up again. My chest hurt. My head was ringing. I felt like I was going to black out.

I was in emotional danger of checking out. I was fighting and flighting. I was a mess!

So I prayed to God. I asked for His help to breathe and to help me center myself in the middle of the anger surging through my mind. My eyes were shut and my hands were wringing. "God, just give me one thing to hold onto." I needed God to anchor my flailing spirit, so that I wouldn't spin out into the universe and never come back. I needed God to layer some other truths on top of my feelings, so I could cope.

I prayed and then I opened my eyes and looked down at my hands. There on my finger was my wedding ring, the one that my husband had picked out. The symbol of our undying love, and yet he was dead. "Lord, this feels like more than I can bear." Yet I tried to stay with the feeling. I stared down at the ring. I felt the aloneness. I felt the widow-ness creeping back into my soul. "Stay with me," God said, urging me to hold onto Him and not fight the anger or run away from it. "Stay, Kristi." Tears filled my eyes and I gazed at my ring through clouds of pain. "God, layer the pain with something else to make it manageable."

Sometimes we see the clearest through tear-filled eyes. My wedding band had three diamonds on it. One of the diamonds on the side was the original gem from our wedding day almost 25 years ago. We had it remounted 15 years later, added an almost identical diamond to the other side and then plopped a new and bigger diamond in the middle of them. Mike and I had been going through a rough patch of life and decided that we would designate the larger diamond in the middle as God.

69

Mike and I were the two smaller diamonds on either side. God was bigger than both of us. Just like the ring, as long as we kept God in the center of our lives we would be okay.

And now with the truth of Mike's death beating loud in my chest, I was angry so I asked God to help me. I prayed that He would heal my heart. Something fluttered inside my chest, and I felt the beginnings of healing as truth trickled in. God was still there between Mike and me. I was realizing that even though many things had changed with his death, some things are eternal.

There are timeless treasures that nothing can take away, not even death. Love is one of them. The love that Mike and I had was unending. His death did not eliminate the love and respect I had for him—it illuminated it. I still loved Michael and probably always would. Even if I chose to marry another man later in life, Michael was the father of our beautiful girls and I spent much of my life happily married to him. I could not be with Mike now. Death separated us physically, but God was still in the center of us and God was still bigger than the two of us. Remembering that our love is eternal took some of the sting of his death away. Mike was gone, but his love would stay with me. Death has no power over love. Love remains even when our loved ones are gone. I could continue to trust God to be bigger than my anger and bigger than Mike's death. The three diamonds had reminded me of this.

The two-step process of Prayer and Layer is one of the highest learnings I have to offer you out of my encounter with grief. Learning how to stay with difficult emotions is a supernatural ability. Prayer brings in the divine help that is needed to stay with anger until it gives way to grace. Layer is allowing God to bring in healing thoughts on top of the anger. Picture a layer cake with stacks of cake and filling and frosting piled high. Prayer, Layer, repeat.

Example Two

I will give another example of the Prayer and Layer process so that you can take a hold of it. I prayed and God layered my pain with new insights until healing came, one layer at a time. Each time I prayed for help and deliberately sat in the discomfort, waiting for God, He met me there. Over time, each inch of anger that I brought to Him received kindness and deep compassion. His love wove together my broken heart with gentleness and tender care. Layering is a delicate process.

Dear Fellow Griever: I am asking for grace as we approach this next example of layering that I am about to cover with you. This is a touchy subject, so hear my heart address this area with the utmost respect and care. Anger is sometimes compounded by mental images that can torture an already wounded heart. I would not be entering this area of grief if I did not have good reason to do so. Bear with me.

Some of us are carrying around mental pictures of our loved ones that evoke anger and cause considerable damage to our hearts. What mental images do you have of your loved one when they died? Death is always dramatic, but also sometimes it is traumatic.

71

If you have experienced a traumatic death of a loved one, then hear my deepest condolences. There are sights and sounds and feelings from the night my husband died that were deeply disturbing. I would have deleted them from my memory if I could have, but I can't. They are etched in my mind. That is why I have used the Prayer and Layer method of coping with these vivid images. You can't erase the trauma, but you can layer it with other memories to soften the impact.

The picture I have in my mind of seeing Mike dead in the driveway has been layered time and time again. Each time the image pops into my mind of that night I carefully add another photo alongside of it. Our wedding photo. Our family portrait. Pictures of us traveling. At the beach with the girls. At the Dayton Dragons game. Layering these photos doesn't eliminate the mental image of him lifeless on the sidewalk, but it counter balances it with photos of adventure and romance and family vacations. It helps the healing.

I don't think it would be fair for the picture of death to overshadow the years of life we had together. I am asking you to do the same process of Prayer and Layer over whatever traumatic mental images you have of your loved one dead or dying. Please apply mental images of your loved one alive and living. This would be especially vital if your loved one died with traumatic circumstances or a prolonged illness that deteriorated them physically. Don't allow their memory to be distorted by their death. Remember their life.

One of the hardest images to incorporate into healing for the girls and me happened on the night that Mike passed. He died at home, and we have vivid memories of seeing Mike's body without his spirit. Michael had always been so full of life and an exuberant personality, so to see him lifeless was shocking to us all.

I bring this subject up because this may be something that is keeping you stuck in anger. It may also be one of your hardest memories to deal with. If you carry that same kind of image in your head of your loved one in a casket, at the hospital, or in declining health, you need layering. We are not able to delete these vivid images from our minds and we can be haunted in nightmares, flashbacks, and mental photographs. Layering diffuses the anger and effectively removes the stinger.

Example Three

It was a huge transition going from being married for a quarter of a century back to being a single woman overnight. At that point in my life I had been a wife for longer than half of my life!? (Wow!!! All of the sudden I feel ancient!!!) Single did not come natural to me and widow was a title I hated, but either way you want to slice it I was no longer a bride. The loneliness was severe. Mike and I had been soulmates and we had this amazing rhythm to our lives.

I had known Mike since I was 15 and we were a good match. We were not identical, but more like a nice set of bookends. I think we kept it all together by leaning toward each other.

73

He kept me up and I kept him up. When Mike died it felt like someone removed the other bookend and all of the sudden my life tumbled down off the mantle on to the floor. Things got crazy!!!

Alone at 48 years old…well not alone, because I had my two girls but at times I certainly felt like I was alone. Mike and I had done so much together and that made his absence all the harder. What I missed most was the way Mike looked at me. His eyes lit up when he was with me or when he talked about me. He saw me. He knew me. I was fully known and fully loved. That was such a gift to my heart. He believed in me. He valued me. So in one sense I missed what we had, but in another sense I longed to have it again. His loss made me long for companionship. I longed for a new husband. I longed for a lover. I longed for someone to see me, value me, and believe in me. I longed to be a bride again. But, you can't become a bride without a groom. At the very least, you need a date! Alas, there was no one. Not anyone I was attracted to. Or was it, no one was attracted to me? I don't know, but I felt like I was the lone single woman in a pool of married couples. I was too young to be a widow, and too old to go clubbing. I was the odd man out. Alone. Lonely. Lost.

The aloneness drove me to madness and I knew I needed to use the 2 step process of Prayer and Layer to help me manage this anger and the longing I had for a new relationship. So I took my heart to Jesus and asked Him in Prayer to help me with this longing. As I sat on my bed and poured out my heart to God He began to whisper to me. He had seen my longing for a husband. He knew that I had been lonely.

He reassured me that my anger was natural and normal, but then he told me something I did not expect to hear.

"You know that I am the true lover of your heart, don't you? There will never be anyone who loves you more than I do. I see you. I value you. I believe in you. You are my forever bride. You may feel lonely but you are never alone. I understand what you are longing for, but do you understand how much I can fill your heart?"

He began to Layer my anger and aloneness with His love for me. "I send you flowers, and gentle breezes, and long beaches to walk. I am the only who made your heart and I am the one who can heal it. Don't look for another man to fill the void. Allow me to love you like you never have before. Walk with Me and talk with Me. Tell Me all about your anger, disappointments, and dreams and secrets.

I will listen anytime.

When the time is right I will bring a new love to you, but until then remain in My love."

God sees my longing. He hears my heart cry. He always will love me. I don't have to long so deeply for someone else because Jesus calls me His bride. God continues to layer on His love to this day. The 2 step process of Prayer and Layer brings in the big guns to help neutralize anger. Every angry or traumatic memory that I have brought to God in prayer and allowed Him to layer has received healing.

Neutralize

Layering is essential to help neutralize the traumatic effect that these angry snapshots have on our hearts. Every time that the image of Mike laying lifeless in the driveway comes into my mind, I use Prayer and Layer. I pray and ask God to help me, and then I allow that mental image to develop in front of me. I don't fight it or take flight from it, but I do call forth other images of Mike to put alongside it. I pull up memories of him smiling and waving to us on his way to work, or fishing, or at a tennis match for Faith, or rooting for Abbi at a cross-country race. Layering is a careful process of allowing the painful image to be directly in front of me, but asking God to help me layer it with other, just as real, but more pleasant images. I don't dismiss the negative image, but I do add other positive images on top of it.

I have found that I typically do not have to prompt angry feelings or painful images. They pop up in my thoughts, dreams, and surroundings. Layering gives me the ability to put the medicine of healing thoughts and images alongside the wounds, and let the process of healing continue. The entire memory of your loved one's life is not meant to be overshadowed by final images of them in a funeral home or hospice bed. Layering allows us to zoom back from that traumatic ending and remember the balance of their whole life.

The quilt is not made up of one final square, but a multitude of memories in glorious harmony. With time and practice, Praying and Layering will become more comfortable to you. My prayers have developed from one-sentence cries for help into meaningful dialogue with the Divine One. I am able to carry on conversations with Him daily. I hear from my Heavenly Father through songs on the radio, beauty in nature, the eyes of a compassionate friend, and meaningful passages in scripture. God is everywhere. Prayer and Layer are ways we can tune into His voice and hear His love. Even books like this one, I hope, will help you hear God's whispers to your hurting heart.

Prayer, Layer, repeat. Applying this simple two-step process will help you move from fighting and flighting your anger and into healing it. When it comes to the heartbreak of grief, we all want to "get it right" so that we can live, truly live.

I hope that these suggestions are helpful to you in absorbing the pain and implementing healing.

War Stories

I know there are all sorts of encounters with grief, so I am careful to listen respectfully when someone shares their story with me. Mostly, I listen. I find people just want to share their story with me, because they know I have had my own encounter with grief. They sense my compassion. Maybe it's like meeting another soldier, you feel freer to share your war stories.

So I have heard lots of stories. People feel free to talk to me and they even tell me things they have never shared with anyone before. They whisper it. I understand this: sometimes saying things out loud makes them more real. Grief is hard to talk about. We have to say things softly, because our own hearts are listening. So we whisper out of respect for the loss and the longing.

77

But sometimes we whisper out of shame. We aren't proud of what we are revealing, so we say it in hushed tones. Grievers speak softly about suicide and homicide, so I listen even more intently. I lean in. I reach out. There is a stigma that keeps grievers from talking openly about this kind of pain. This should not be. Let it not be so.

Secret Sorrow

If you have a loved one that has died of suicide or homicide, I am so sorry. Your pain is riddled with questions that I cannot answer, and that even you may not be able to answer. Maybe no one can answer. I don't have answers, but I care for your pain. I want you to know that God has heard your whispers, and that He sees your pain. Your grief may be hidden to those around you, but God sees your secret sorrow.

I have written this entire book with a holy dependence on God to speak through me. As I approach this subject of suicide and homicide, I have asked God to speak for me. I have no words of comfort of my own. I entrust the Holy Spirit to speak for me. I shut my own mouth and allow Him to speak to your heart. Here is what I hear Him saying to you.

Listen Closely

God holds a special place in His heart for you. Your pain is ever before Him and He grieves for you and with you. His eyes are on you and His hand rests on you now even as you grieve.

78

God leans into you and wraps you in His warm embrace. You are safe in His arms.

Whatever it is that has caused you such extreme grief, He knows. He is aware of your questions and troubling thoughts. He has words of comfort that He longs to speak to you directly. Spend time with God in prayer.

Tell Him your frustration, your intense anger, your hidden rage. He is listening and He cares for you deeply.

God is close to the broken-hearted and He is close to you now. Feel his presence. Lean into His chest. Allow His loving arms to wrap around you and hold you. He wants to bring healing to your broken heart.

Release the anger that you have been hiding and allow His grace to flood your heart. Let His healing light illuminate your pain. Trust His gentle hands to guide you through this valley. He knows the way to lead you through this dark night of the soul. Commit yourself to spending time in His presence daily. Give Him your anxious thoughts. Rest in His care. Determine to be completely open and honest with God. Do not withhold anything from Him. Bare your soul to the Healer and trust Him to bring you peace. He loves you. He has the power over life and death and He will give you new life.

Grief Counseling

One of the best gifts you can give to your friends and family and to yourself is to heal. If you are struggling to heal, get help. I mean it: get help.

I have seen too many people walking around in pain, because they are too afraid to ask for help. Don't let anything keep you from living. Swallow your pride and take your medicine. Do what it takes to get better. The world needs you; your family needs you. And whether you know it or not, you need healing. Mike and I had a motto, "Drugs, surgery, or whatever it takes to get healthy." I hope that you will do whatever it takes to get healing.

Easter in Your Soul

Do you believe that Jesus rose from the dead? Do you have faith that He overcame death in His own life? Do you think that He can bring Easter into your soul? These are all questions that will help you to determine what you really believe about life and death and life again. If you have not wrestled with these questions before, you will most certainly wrestle with them now that you have experienced loss or you are struggling with a longing.

I invite you to examine your beliefs. Be honest about what you believe and search for answers to your questions about life, death, loss, and longing. Jesus is the answer to your most troubling heart questions. He has the power to lead you into life after death; even the death of your loved one. He has the power to give you life even while you are longing. He wants to give you new life. Explore the possibly of life after loss, even while you long for life to be different.

Prayer for Removing the Stinger

Dear Lord,

I pray to You now for all the broken living among us. For the hidden anger buried deep within. Lord, we beseech You to bring new life where grief has dampened our souls and loss has left us listless. Breathe life into our dry bones and create in us new awareness of life.

There is a stinger that has irritated us to the point of anger. Something has deeply affected us and wounded us profoundly. We grieve and rage against the loss or longing that is infecting our lives now.

We need You to help us remove the stinger. Help us locate the source of our anger and neutralize its negative influence so that we unlock that anger that holds our hearts captive.

When triggers pop up that threaten our mental health, we ask You to bring healing images to mind. When we fall victim to our anger, enable us to process these emotions and move through this grief process.

Lord, we have been in the anger stage long enough. We long to leave this desert place and drink from Your fountain of everlasting life. We are thirsty for living water. Our mouths are parched with grief and we crave the bread of life.

Sustain our broken hearts and deliver our spirits to the place of healing. We long for You. Hear our prayer, Oh Lord. We ask You to fill us with hope. Turn Your ear to hear our cry. Come to where we are and lead us to Your heart. Through Christ, who made the way for us to live in You, we ask these things. Amen.

81

Chapter 3

Embrace Awkward:
Unlock Sadness

Sometimes, sadness is hard to distinguish from anger. Both are intense emotions and especially in the grief process. Some people have a hard time admitting their sadness. I know that I do. It's much easier for me to feel angry than to feel sad. Anger feels powerful, commanding, and in charge; while sadness feels weak, vulnerable, and overpowering. Some people will react with anger even when they are sad. This seems like an odd expression, but I think sadness and anger are hard to differentiate at times.

I know people whose "go to" emotion is anger. When they are sad, it reveals as anger. When they are lonely, it reveals as anger. When they are threatened emotionally, they react with anger. It's as if they have one notch on the emotional dial and everything points to anger.

Anger can masquerade as a variety of emotions, including sadness. Anger can cloak the real emotion of sadness and make it difficult to determine what you are actually feeling. Be sure to examine your emotions a little more closely.

Often times, grievers can hide sadness under the umbrella of anger. Picture sorting through your emotions like sorting your laundry: Just imagine piles of clothes – whites, darks, and delicates. Sort through your emotions and start dividing them up into three piles – denial, anger, and sadness. When we throw all our laundry together without sorting, the dark colors can bleed into the whites. Without sorting your emotions, denial and anger will bleed into sadness.

To help you distinguish sadness from the other grief emotions, I will give you an idea of what to look for in this stage of grief. Sadness slows you down and weighs on your heart. Sadness can show up from regret, disappointment, broken dreams, discouragement, and unmet expectations.

You entered denial, have processed some of your anger, and now move into sadness. Sadness is a natural byproduct of grief. I was not surprised to feel sad about the death of my husband. That was appropriate. What did surprise me was the depth of sadness I felt during this particular stage of grief. Sadness had woven into my life since Mike passed, but now sadness descended like a heavy veil. Sadness ran though my veins like lead. I felt deep sorrow.

This profound sadness was unlike any I had ever experienced before. Everyday tasks were now laborious. My limbs felt like they were weighed down, my muscles were drained of strength. Even my emotions felt heavier. I had entered the sadness and it scared me. Would I make it out? Would I ever feel right again? Would I be able to laugh and smile without so much effort? Sadness was debilitating.

You will know you are in the sadness stage of grieving when you feel like you are walking in ankle high mud. Every step takes concerted effort. You may feel heaviness in your eyes as if your forehead were dropping down into your eyebrows. I felt sad. Deeply sad. It might even scare you to be this sad.

Quicksand

These pockets of uncertainty and doubt were like quicksand for my soul. The more I wrestled, the more my spirit sunk down into the mess. Panic overcame me and I wanted to go running out of the mud, but my struggle only left me deeper embedded into the mire. Stuck. Stranded.

I hated the feeling. Helpless. Alone. It sucked! Grief had me tired. And I began to wonder, would I make it out? Would there be a time when I was not hurting? Would I be able to survive this endless struggle? Where was the finish line? When would I get to cross over it and throw my arms up in victory? When would I get to feel somewhat happy again?

Now, don't get me wrong, I had occasional moments of happiness when laughter spilled out of my mouth and filled the air. But the majority of the time I was pushing to keep up with the daily tasks of life, all the while carrying a huge bag of sorrow. Sorrow is heavy; it doesn't take much sorrow to weigh us down. My heart felt stuck.

The Only Way

My goal was to get through the pain, discomfort, and profound sadness and get to the place of healing, restoration, and wholeness, so I revisited my options. There was no way in my mind I could go back to the way things were before my husband died, because frankly, my husband was dead. There was also no way I wanted to stay in the extreme anxiety and uncomfortableness of the grieving widow stage.

85

There seemed to be only one viable option...to ask God to help me rebuild my life. The reality of the burnt bridge behind me made me more aware that I had to find a new way. I needed God to show me a fresh path.

Through the Valley

The old, sacred Psalm 23 became my transformation mantra. Here I was, quite literally in the valley of the shadow of death. Afraid, somewhat lost, and not knowing what to do, I turned to the Lord as my shepherd.

He would get me through this. He would lead me to quiet places and refreshing spaces. He would feed me and lead me and guide me through this valley. I had not experienced death myself, but the shadow of death was all around me. This shadow, this dark area beside death, was scary and I would need a trusted, experienced guide to get me through this low place. The Lord was with me: He would not let me be lost. He would lead me through the valley.

This historic Psalm, written thousands of years ago, became my new song. I would meditate on the truths contained in the verses and they became medicine for my aching soul. Beyond music, and meditation, and medicine...these words were instructions for me. I would talk to God all day long and ask Him simple questions like when to eat, when to take a nap, when to walk, when to rest. And I was led.

Guided

God's spirit would speak to me. I would be so exhausted and not know if I should eat something or lay down. I would hear in my inner ear that I should eat something first and then lay down for a nap. Again, I would ask the next thing to do. Should I make this phone call or sit down to pay bills? And again I would be led. I learned not only to rely on my Guide for the big overwhelming tasks, but I also learned to lean into Him for the simple, everyday, routine decisions.

The Lord was my shepherd and He was restoring my soul. He was leading me through the valley of the shadow of death and I was becoming less afraid every day.

When fear mounted up against me I remembered this simple phrase: "The Lord is my shepherd." I am not ashamed to admit that I became completely and utterly dependent on Him.

Shadows

Every day, God showed up with His love and light and every day He led me. As the time passed, I was able to see that the shadow of death was getting shorter. Shadows are long when the sun is the furthest away. The sun comes up over the horizon and as the sun moves across the sky and more overhead, the shadows lose their length. As I allowed the light of God to move closer to my heart, the shadow of death got shorter. My goal became to be so surrounded by God's light that the shadow of death would be swallowed up in His glorious light.

87

His love would neutralize my loss and all that would remain would be love. This was becoming my new reality.

Grief is a Cocoon

Grief changes us. It reminds me of the caterpillar and the butterfly. The caterpillar is who we are before grief. Grief is like the cocoon that the caterpillar is wrapped up in for a season. The butterfly is what emerges after grief. Grief has changed us; we are no longer caterpillars. That former part of us changed. Grief is really the beginning of a new life. A life with wings! We are not completely changed in this transformation: the butterfly still has the head and body of a caterpillar. But going through this grief experience has given the previous caterpillar amazing, colorful, magnificent butterfly wings.

Who I was before Mike died does resemble who I am now, but there is a dramatic difference. I am a familiar resemblance to the old Kristi with an undoubtedly strange new twist. Grief changes us. I believe grief is meant to change us, and change us for the better. There is a gift in the cocoon…wings. There is a gift in grief…new life. Having gone through this cocoon of grief, I am able to emerge with gifts and abilities that I did not possess before.

Wings

How does the caterpillar get its wings? The caterpillar gets its beautiful butterfly wings by simply submitting to the process of change. Have you ever thought about what would happen if the caterpillar simply refused to enter the cocoon? Can you blame him? The cocoon is dark, and the caterpillar will be all alone. I am sure it will be uncomfortable and cramped all wrapped up like that. How will he survive? But the caterpillar trusts the Creator and he trusts the process of transformation. If the caterpillar submits to the changes, he becomes a butterfly.

Can we learn from the caterpillar and submit to the cocoon of grief? Do we trust the Creator? Do we trust the grief process? Don't refuse the cocoon of grief. Transformation happens in the dark seasons of our lives.

Yield to the Creator and allow Him to re-create your life.

Embracing change, admitting awkwardness, allowing for vulnerability can be challenging even in the best of circumstances. It can be exceptionally threatening when you are thrown off balance by the loss or longing. But it has been my experience that finding balance again requires the courage to be okay with being off balance for a while. To find center, you have to recognize the areas where you are off center and go about the task of creating balance.

Grief seems to throw everything off: who you were is no longer who you are. What you did before does not feel the same for you now. Where you went, who you spent time with, how you managed before is all affected, because you are not the same. Everything feels different. Everything has changed.

Going back to the way things were is impossible, but moving forward is scary. Standing still is uncomfortable. So what do you do?

How do you sort through what was and how do we move forward into what will be? How do we assimilate what has happened so that we can learn and grow and become? There is really one way through it. This will sound redundant - but the only way through it...is through it.

God-Wings

I have been going through a life transition much like that of a caterpillar transforming into a butterfly. The process started about a year ago when I felt God wrapping me up in a cocoon and asking me to trust Him in the process. Recently, I was able to emerge from my temporary changing-chamber to behold these glorious, colorful God-wings. I was no longer a caterpillar; I was a butterfly. WOW! I was so excited to fly, to try out these new wings, but God gently reminded me that these new wings still needed time to dry. So while I waited and rested, God placed in my former caterpillar mind that I should go ahead and start dreaming about the places I would like to go and the things I would like to see. God was inviting me to let my spirit soar while my body prepared for flight.

As I sat in the sun, I dreamed of writing a book. A book that asked the question, "How is your heart?" A written testimony about the ability that God has to take our hearts, no matter what condition they are in, and give them new life. This book would be a tribute to God, who has transformed and awakened my heart. It would be a bold reminder that God has the power to help us rise above anything that we face here on Earth.

It would be my anthem to the Lifter of all human hearts. With God's blessing I began to write and He has certainly been with me in this endeavor.

How is Your Heart?

The God of the universe wants to know..."How is your heart?" Take a moment and think about how you would answer that question. Be honest. God is gently waiting for your answer: God wants to know because He cares for you. He wants to speak to your heart with words of comfort, compassion, and peace. God wants to remind us of the truth - that He can give our hearts wings. He wants desperately to infuse our minds with dreams and visions of a transcendent life. God longs to lift us to new heights of thinking and relating and being.

Will we trust God to do what we will never be able to do on our own power? Will we allow Him to raise us above our circumstances, beyond our limitations, and over ourselves? Will we believe that inside every caterpillar is a set of wings waiting to burst forth? Will we allow God to give our hearts wings?

Change

Change has happened. One of the best things we can do is talk about the changes. One of the worst things we can do is not talk about them. When the people around you expect you to carry on as normal when nothing is normal anymore, it can add to the pain.

If you expect yourself to be able to carry on as normal when everything hurts, it can heap on the hurt.

Talk About It

Talk about what is weighing your heart down. Speak it out loud. If you have experienced the death of a friend or family member, talk about your loved one. The girls and I will tell each other how we are feeling. "I miss Dad." "I hate that he's not here to see this." "I know he would love to see how you are growing up." "He would be so proud of you." We talk about him even though he is not here. Do you talk about your loved one? Can you share funny stories about times that you had with them? Can you be honest with the times they got on your nerves? Talking about your loved one can help with the sadness.

At family gatherings, are you able to acknowledge that someone is missing? Are your family and friends open to talking about your feelings or do they avoid the subject? Can you talk about the awkwardness of being in a familiar setting without someone you held dear being there? Can they cry with you? Do they ask you how you are doing and do they share how they are doing related to the death?

In the case of longing for something you do not have, it is just as important to talk about this grief. Confide in friends and family members – tell them how hard it is for you to pick out a Father's Day card for the man that is your biological father, but has never been a dad to you. All the cards are geared for close meaningful relationships, but you haven't talked with your dad in two years. He hasn't sent you a birthday or Christmas card in more years than that. You wish you had a dad who showed more interest in your life. You long for it, but it is just not true.

Express Your Sadness

If you express your sadness in healthy ways, you will be better able to move through the sadness. Sadness lifts as you are able to express the sadness. Allow yourself to do something that helps move the pain out of your heart. Whatever allows you to feel the sadness and then let it out is what you need to do. I might make a fire in the fireplace that my husband built on our patio and have some quiet time thinking back through all the crazy things we did together. I could remember the times he could irritate me, or wonderful times when we would sit at this same fireplace together. You might:

- Talk about it to one of your friends who understands
- Write about it in your journal
- Join a support group
- Take a course on "grief care" through your local church or community center
- Paint a picture
- Read the sympathy cards you received early in the grief process
- Sit with your sadness beside a roaring fire outside
- Take your sadness fishing

93

- Put on your nasty old sweatshirt and sit on the couch for the weekend
- Put a stone with the date of your loved one's passing carved in it in your garden
- Plant your mother-in-law's favorite tree
- Go to an auto show your dad would have loved and think of him as you walk through the cars
- Take a trip to a spot you visited with your wife and be thankful for the time you had with her

This may sound weird to you, but sometimes I talk to my dead husband. It helps me feel connected to him in spirit. I tell him how much I miss him. I tell him how the girls are doing and that we had his favorite meal the other night (meatloaf...that man loved meatloaf!). Talking, building a fire, and remembering are all ways that I process my sadness.

Change is awkward for everyone involved. Let's be brave enough to acknowledge the awkwardness out loud with each other. Let's be honest enough to say how we are hurting. And let's be vulnerable enough with each other to say the obvious. Change is awkward. Embrace awkward.

D=Dare to Dream
R=Remove the Stinger
E=Embrace Awkward

Key to Unlock Sadness: Embrace "Awkward"

I was going to tell you that the key to overcoming sadness was to embrace change, but that phrase has been used a lot lately and seemed redundant. Change has happened, whether we've welcomed it or not. We are in the cocoon. Change occurred; we had no say in it and no vote. It just happened. What we do have control over is how we approach the changes that entered our existence. This is where the "embracing" can happen, and needs to, so that growth can result. We can embrace the awkwardness of the changes.

We can make friends with the loneliness. We can hug the hurt. We can make peace with the pain. We can be proactive in doing what will help move us forward. Reacting to the changes in ways that build character and friendships and family. Pursuing positive interactions with friends and family that propel us toward healing.

After Mike died, it was awkward for me to go out with the two couples that Mike and I used to go out with together. I was single now, a widow showing up alone for dinner with married people. I felt odd sitting there by myself and trying to carry on conversation. It felt strange to sit with the same friends, but without Mike. I knew I would never get over the sadness if I didn't do what was uncomfortable.

Admitting Awkward

The same thing happened at family gatherings. I felt awkward, but I did not want to miss the

95

family time with brothers, sisters, cousins, and grandparents. It was really awkward to be there without my husband, their dad, their brother, their uncle, their son. We all had to be honest with how hard it was without Mike, but also be mindful that we still had each other. Sadness was evident. Change was apparent. It was awkward, uncomfortable, and hard. But we chose to embrace awkward and embrace each other.

Those first few holidays are hard on the grieving. It's the holidays and you would normally be happy, but this year you are sad. That first birthday, Thanksgiving, Christmas, or anniversary can be miserably uncomfortable and downright depressing. Feel the sadness, talk about it, and express it. Grace is required. Hugs and tears and gentle words go a long way towards healing. Kind gestures and compassionate comments usher in the comfort to help with the loss. Give grace in spades to the other grievers and ask for grace for yourself. Lavish on love. Respect your boundaries and the boundaries of others. And rest. Get lots of rest. You deserve it.

Getting over the sadness only happens when you allow yourself to feel the full extent of the sorrow and take the uncomfortable steps to overcome it. The last thing you want to do is remain sad. So feel it all, to the depths of your sadness. Go low, so you can reach the bottom and then start the journey back up. Be honest with yourself about how you really feel. Be honest with others about how this is affecting you.

It was hard for me to admit that I was not going to be able to stay at Mike's family homestead for Thanksgiving and Christmas. I was too broken; my nerves could not handle it.

I knew I needed to stay at a hotel so we would be able to come and go as needed during the day. Seeing all the family for extended time during those first high emotion-filled days would have been exhausting! I did not have the bandwidth to be around people for more than three to four hours at one time.

I had to embrace the awkwardness of saying that I needed to go back to the hotel to rest. We were all grieving heavily and we all had different needs. I had to be honest with what I needed and hope they would understand. The last thing you need as a griever is more pressure; you need friends and family that support you and give room to manage the emotions of grieving.

Some people will understand and some won't. Some will make it more awkward and some will relieve the tension. But no matter what other people do, it will be awkward. Change is always awkward. Embrace it.

Life After Loss

There is life after death. Not only do I believe there is life after death for the person who has died, I also believe there is life after death for those of us left here on Earth. For the griever, there is life for you after the death of your spouse, parent, child, or other loved one.

Do you believe in this kind of life after death? I will be honest; I do believe that a piece of me died with my husband that night. Parts of my daughters died that October evening when they saw their father die in the driveway. But I also believe with all my heart that something was born in us when

Mike died. I believe that his death has given new life to his girls and me. Mike's seeds of love and joy and faith were planted in our hearts when he died. We are not the same people we were before he died.

I have noticed a difference in Mike's friends and family too. It is like parts of Mike's personality were distributed when he died. Gifts were granted to his grievers: maybe Mike deposited something into our hearts. I have seen glimpses of Mike in the people he loved. They are stronger, clearer, more relaxed, more confident, and they rely on God like never before. It's like Mike's spirit was shared among the mourners. Not his soul—Mike's soul went to live in heaven with God. But I see reflections of Mike's spirit all around me. When Mike died, some sort of spiritual gifting happened, a sacred exchange. I believe parts of Mike live on in the people he touched. We have been changed for the better. There is life after death, even when the loss is the death of a loved one.

Life While Longing

There is life while longing. When we ache for things, we have a preoccupation with what is missing and this is a gentle reminder to look around. Focusing on what we don't have can leave us lopsided in our thinking and we tend to stress about those matters most.

Breathe. Count your blessings. Don't let the longing make you blind to all of the good things you do have. Put it all into perspective. Obsessing about what we don't have can make us forget all we do have.

Don't let that one piece you long for make you bitter and negative about your whole life. I think this next story will remind us to keep things in perspective and keep looking forward. Remember to enjoy the life you have even as you long for more.

Feel But Don't Feed

Similar to every other stage of grief it is important to feel the feelings, but be careful not to feed them. Do you understand what I mean by feeling them, but not feeding them? In order to get through the grief and get to the healing, we are required to feel the emotions of each stage. But like the sign says in the park, "Do not feed the bears," I would remind you, "Do not feed the feelings."

There is a slight, but profound, difference between feeling the sadness and feeding the sadness. The difference really has to do with hope. Hope is what allows us to be sad for a season without making sadness a permanent state of mind. Do you hear me on this? Sadness is one of the steps that leads to healing, but don't be deceived that sadness is terminal.

You may be afraid to feel sad, because you don't want to be depressed.

Depression, to me, is when you have experienced something that you have not been able to process and it shuts you down. Depression happens when you feel hopeless.

An longing, loss, or death presses on your heart - in other words, it leaves a mark.

99

That Girl...Awkward!

Okay...this story is too funny not to share! I am calling it THAT GIRL. This is a true story and it happened to me. Talk about AWKWARD! It was about one year after Mike died, and I was in that awkward stage of trying to go out socially again. Only this time, it was as a single lady. I was not feeling comfortable with my new found "freedom." I certainly did not feel free – I felt more like the awkward girl at the school dance. Social settings felt like junior high all over again. One night, I was at a birthday party with my best friend. There were lots of people there. The house was gorgeous, like something out of a magazine. The crowd there was sophisticated, but not stuffy. There were all adults and no kids. This was a catered event with two bartenders and a table full of yummy finger foods and desserts. Somehow, I just knew this was going to be lots of fun!

My friend and I only knew the host and about five other people there. So we were mingling, meeting new people, eating, drinking, and laughing. We got a tour of the house and then we ended up hanging out downstairs with our friends. We were in this huge downstairs where there was a media room, bar, and again...lots of people. Did I mention lots of people?

My best friend went into the bathroom and then she came back out. We were standing there talking to the host's mom for a while and then I went into the bathroom. I had started to close the door when I realized there was no lock. That made me a little nervous, but I knew my best friend was standing right outside the door, so I thought I was safe. Surely she would stand guard for me.

I sat down and started to do what I came in there to do, when all of the sudden the door opened and this good looking man walked about half way in the bathroom. He looked at me, and I looked at him and I instinctively reached out to try and close the door. There was this incredibly awkward moment when we both realized what had just happened and we just stared at each other. We both had that wide-eyed look of terror and surprise on our faces. He slowly backed out and then finally closed the door. I just sat there...laughing...and in shock...and I could not believe what just happened to me!

Hide or Seek

A life lesson I learned on the toilet is...you can hide or seek. When we were kids we played "Hide and Seek" and that was a fun game.

But games aside, life presents us with opportunities to hide *or* seek.

We can hide. I could have stayed in the bathroom until all the people left the party and then come out. I could have avoided some of the embarrassment, but I would have also missed the party. God doesn't want you to miss the party. When uninvited events enter our life, we need to allow God to lead us. We all need safe people around us to help process what just happened and help us move on. When you can get to the point where you can laugh at yourself, you can let in so much healing.

101

We can hide, or we can seek. Instead of staying in that awkward, defensive position and never leaving the bathroom, I chose to go on the offensive and make a new plan.

I gathered myself together, finished the paperwork, and heard this random intruder laughing right outside the door with my best friend. Well, at that moment she was my EX best friend because she was supposed to be standing guard for me. Then I washed my hands and tried to pull myself together. As I looked in the mirror, I realized that I would have to leave the bathroom and see this man again. I took a deep breath and bravely came out to face my embarrassment. My friend was right there and we started howling with laughter! Luckily, the man was nowhere to be seen. I was sure he had disappeared upstairs to avoid the even more awkward moment of "Oh, hi...I just saw you sitting on the john!"

You can say, "Okay, this awful thing happened to me, but I am going to seek out ways to make the most of it and even have some fun." It is so much a matter of taking what happens to us and making the most of it. Sometimes it's easier than others, but I think it is important to capture and capitalize on whatever we can. Seek out opportunities to leverage what has happened to you and allow God to turn your mess into memories.

Seek God. Seek answers. Seek solutions. Seek, don't hide.

I was initially relieved to not see this man when I came out of the bathroom. But then I realized there was no way I was going to be able to avoid running into the man at this party, so I went in search of him. It was a "face your fears or they become bigger" kind of a thing. I spotted him upstairs and I walked directly up to him and introduced myself. I thought that I should at least know the name of the man who just saw me in such a personal position!

Turned out, he's single...and a cop! He was a nice guy, and we were able to laugh about our brief encounter. Laughter makes most things bearable. I had never met him before, but talking to him I found out that I had known his aunt for years (and she still goes to church with me). I knew his cousin from years ago when Mike and I were youth pastors. Small world. My friend, who was now my best friend again, immediately put several notes on the bathroom door reminding people to "knock before entering" and the "door does not lock." Hopefully this would keep this from happening to someone else, but if it didn't...I hoped they had a best friend to help them laugh at themselves like I did. Word got out at the party about the downstairs bathroom having no lock and that some guy walked in on a lady while she was seated on the throne. Stories like this one tend to spread like wildfire...so the rest of the evening when I met people they would say, "Oh, you are THAT girl!" Yes...I am THAT girl...the girl that got caught with her pants down by a perfect stranger who just happened to be a good-looking, single cop. THAT GIRL!

Oh...and for those of you who are wondering if this single man and I saw more of each other...I think he saw enough!

Potty Parable

You see, this man had a vision of me that I couldn't delete from his mind. He saw that I don't wad my toilet paper into a ball, but fold it gently. How many people in your life know such intimate details about you? Well, now you all know because I told you! But I can do nothing to change the past. I am powerless to erase what happened. I must Embrace Awkward. I have decided to employ my tactic in dealing with this sudden embarrassment as a life lesson. What can be learned from this potty parable? There are several lessons I learned that evening.

Shame and Blame

The first lesson that I learned that night has to do with shame and blame. I chose not to shame this accidental intruder...or blame my friend - my best friend - for not standing guard to keep him from busting in. Shame and blame are not going to do anything but cause more hurt. I could charge the police officer with "breaking and entering" and shame him. The door was closed. The word "toilet" was stenciled on the door right at his eye level. What was he thinking to open it without knocking? Of course, I did "throw the book at him" all in fun, but no real shaming happened.

And what about Michele, my best friend: where was she when I needed her? Well, she was sitting down on the job. Literally: sitting right there on the couch, not three feet from the bathroom door. She had just gone to the bathroom and she knew there was no lock on the door. She had meant to tell me when she came out of the bathroom, but then we got distracted talking to the host's mom who had a cute sweater and she forgot. Michele had meant to tell me and it slipped her mind.

Michele had positioned herself on guard close to the door and was watching out for me. She saw two people walking toward the door, but they went on by. When this man started to walk by, she assumed he was following the others until he suddenly turned and opened the door. All she could do was gasp as he grabbed the door handle and pushed. It all happened so fast.

I could blame Michele for not keeping her full attention on the bathroom door in case someone came along and didn't knock before entering, but we were at a party. The music was loud, there were a lot of characters for fun people-watching, and I know her heart. This woman has shown up for me like no one else in the past two years of grief. Michele has texted me every day, usually several times a day. She has taken me out when I needed to laugh, talk, and get out of the house. She has spent endless evenings on my patio, letting me talk through the many emotions of grief. She even helped me with my daughter's wedding - during tax season - which is her crazy time as a tax accountant. When they were playing the wrong song for Abbi to walk down the aisle, Michele even ran down the aisle and got them to put on the right song.

Michele is my best friend: she has been better to me than I could have ever imagined. Do I want to blame her for the That Girl incident? No. Michele is the one that invited me to the party in the first place.

I wouldn't have been there having all that fun, eating all that fabulous food, and meeting all those new friends if she hadn't invited me. So there is no way, after all that she has done for me, and all the times she has shown up for me, that I was going to blame her. As friends, we chose to laugh about it and make the most of it. And that is why she is my best friend. Isn't that what we all need? Someone to make us laugh and help us make the most out of life's awkward situations? So...no shame, no blame.

Heal First, Help Second

Another lesson I learned from this potty parable, when all my dignity was on display, is that in order to help others, you have to heal yourself first. You have to make it out of the situation yourself before you can help someone else. Once I was able to look in the mirror, take a deep breath, and move through the emotions of what happened, I was able to go re-enter the party. I was able to go back and help Michele put signs on the bathroom door to warn others. If I had not been able to process what happened to me in a healthy way, and instead either hid in the bathroom or left the party, then I would not have been able to help others. Much like writing this book, I have had to go through grief first before I could offer help to you. I have had to go through the seasons of grief one step at a time, and now I am able to leave a bread-crumb trail for you to follow out of darkness and into light.

We are never quite sure why things happen the way they do, but this silly bathroom story has reminded me that I have done my work. I have been able to take a

much more serious trial than a bathroom intrusion—
the death of my dearly loved husband—and using the
same process have been able to grow from what has
happened to me. I am stronger for having gone
through such pain and I think you will be, too.

One day you may find yourself as "That Girl."
You may be "That Man" whose wife left him, or
"That Mom" whose child died, or "That Dad"
who lost his job, or "That Child" whose parents
had an ugly divorce.

Whatever situation you find yourself in,
remember that you will get through it. Choose not
to shame or blame. Decide to not hide, but seek.
And choose to help yourself through, so that you
can then turn around and help others. If you
choose not to hide, but seek, you will be
transformed in the process.

Do What You Can't

Sadness is a stage of grief, but it is not meant to
be a permanent state. On my grief journey, sadness
was the valley, the lowest point. I definitely did not
want to stay stuck in sadness, but I did not know
how to get through the sadness. The key that
unlocked sadness for me was to Embrace
Awkward. What does that actually mean?

Embrace Awkward means to do the thing you
don't think you can do. Go to that party, dance at
that wedding, ask for her phone number, have the
tests run, send out your resume, move to the city,
go to a different church, join that support group,
try the treatments, say goodbye, say hello, travel
out of town or out of the country, say "I love
you," say it again, say it again.

107

Do what you don't think you can do. You don't have to do it well. You probably won't be impressive, but do it anyway. Do it awkward. Do it fumbling. Do it failing or falling. Do it scared, but do it. Don't hold back. Don't shrink back. Give it your all. And smile.

Smile, because you did what you didn't think you could do. Take off the wedding band. Pack the baby clothes away. Meet an old friend for coffee. Meet a new friend for drinks. Open the blinds. Let the light in. Let your fears out. Forgive.

When you are stuck in sadness, it's because you think you will never be happy again or ever be happy without. But that is a lie. Sadness is a season. When it's time, say farewell to sadness. Unlock the handcuffs. I have given you the key. You are free, my friend.

Most people say, "Just do what you can." I say, "Do what you can't!"

I have found it is the daring that makes the difference. The key to unlock sadness is to Embrace Awkward.

Time to Fly

I have decided to trust God and He is proving Himself trustworthy. He has given my heart wings. Please pray for me to allow God to take me to new highs and unseen places and to be brave enough to Embrace Awkward. My wings are dry now. It is time for me to fly. I still don't know exactly where I am going, but I am trusting God to continue to guide me. I am praying for your heart to have wings, for God to grant you healing for your aching heart, and for you to be able to join me in this next phase of life with wings of hope.

Dear God, I am amazed at Your ability to transform hearts. We bring You our broken hearts and ask You to fix them; we have nowhere else to turn.

You are the Healer of hearts that have been ravaged by grief and sadness. You are the One strong enough to bind up our brokenness and gentle enough to be tender in the process. We submit our sadness to You and invite You to lead us to healing. We thank You, in advance, for transforming our hearts and giving us heart-wings. Through Jesus, we ask these things of You. Amen.

Chapter 4

Ask for Help:
Unlock Bargaining

Bargaining is the final phase of grief before acceptance. Bargaining is a more subtle stage of grief to pinpoint; it is not as obvious as anger and sadness and you may not even be aware you are in it. I was only mildly aware of it as I was going through it, and I became more aware of bargaining in hindsight. Let me explain how I understand the bargaining phase and see if you can recognize any of the feelings in your own grief.

What is bargaining? When I think of bargaining, I think of some of the European marketplaces where buyers are expected to haggle over the sale with the seller—much different from our traditional American shopping experiences in malls and large stores where merchandise always has a price tag. In contrast, these Eastern stands have no price point, and even if they do have a price shown, it is understood that there will still be some bargaining before the final sale.

Bargaining has to do with the buyer and the seller coming to an agreement on a fair price for the goods. This is typically a back-and-forth exchange of ideas of the worth of the items before coming to an agreement. The seller has an idea of what the product's value is and the buyer has his own version of the same. The two must agree on a fair market price, otherwise the bargaining continues or the buyer does not get the desired product and the seller does not get the desired sale.

Now, I am not a good bargainer, but I am an awesome bargain shopper. As a decorator for twenty years I prided myself in being able to find the best decorating goods at the lowest prices. I shopped all the name brand discount stores and looked for the best deals for my clients. I called it "Discount decorating at its finest!" It was like treasure hunting, because I had to really sift through a lot of merchandise to find the treasures. It was well worth it, because I could save clients a lot of money and give their home or office a great look and feel.

Haggling

I love to bargain shop, but if I have to haggle with someone over a price, I won't. Luckily, the prices are clearly marked on my decorative treasures; otherwise I could not be a professional shopper. I would not be able to argue with another person, which is why I hate car shopping! Just show me the bottom line price and I will determine if that is a fair price for me. Do not tell me that you have to "talk to your manager" and see what he can do for me. It leaves too much room for confusion.

What will your price for this car be to the next person that walks in the door? Or what about the last time you sold this same car—did the other person pay more or less than you are asking me to pay?

This is exactly why I bought a Saturn for my first new car purchase. Saturn's philosophy was that all its cars would have the price point clearly marked on the window of the car and you would pay the same as every other person would. No haggling, no guesswork, no high-pressure sales. I loved this, because I knew that Saturn was consistent across the board with its prices. If I liked the price and agreed with the amount it had on the window, sold! I loved this new car shopping experience, because it was hassle free and I loved my new car. This Saturn was my first new car and it was beautiful! It had a white exterior, tan leather interior with wood trim accents, and a sunroof. I was styling! The problem today is that Saturn is no longer around—it went out of business. I guess Americans do like to haggle over car prices more than I do. Go figure.

Well, whether you like to haggle or not, you will probably do some haggling in the bargaining phase of grief. Even this old gal was found bargaining. Let me explain.

After grief takes you through denial and shock, drags you through anger, and slides you through sadness, you may be a little spent. You have gone through so much already and you may find yourself, like I did, expecting some payment for all your time and trouble. Life owes me after what I have had to endure. I gave THAT up, God, and so now you owe me THIS. I am not going to do what you want me to do, God, until you make up for what you did to me.

Now, I am not proud of these thoughts, but I have to be honest with you, myself, and God. I thought it was time for God to reimburse me for my pain and suffering.

113

"You took my husband, now find me another one." "I will do what you say, God, but what is in it for me?" And I began to bargain with God.

Entitlement

At this stage of grief I think I had an entitlement mentality: God owed me, and He better pay up - or else. Or else I won't do what He says I should do! Like a little two-year-old I was throwing tantrums, holding my breath, expecting to hurt God. Who was I really hurting? Myself. And why did I want to hurt God? I didn't want to necessarily hurt God; I just wanted Him to reimburse me for my hurt.

I had paid enough, now it was time for God to pay me back—He owed me. In my grieving mind, I said that God better make it up to me...with interest. If He took my husband, He better get me a new one, and fast. And while He was at it, this husband had better be an upgrade. I was demanding payment and restoration. I had rights! I was threatening God. He had better do what I say!

Who did I think I was to be telling God how to make it up to me? But that is exactly where I was.

Arguing With God

I distinctly remember several sparring rounds with God. One Sunday morning in particular stands out for me. I was getting ready for church and arguing with God in the shower. You see, I was going to one church on a regular basis and yet, this Sunday morning I felt God asking me to go to another church. It was a church that I was very familiar with and I knew lots of people there, but I just didn't like God telling me what to do. Haven't I done enough already? Do I really need to go to THAT church THIS morning?

I felt God clearly sending a "Yes." He wanted me to go to that church this morning. "Well, then," my rebuttal was. "Will I meet my new husband? Will he be there this morning?"

"No."

"Are you sure?"

"Yes."

"So, you are saying that you want me to go to this other church, but I will not meet my new husband there today?"

"That's what I am asking you to do."

"Well, I don't want to do it!"

"That is your choice. I am just asking you to trust Me."

I think at this point I was slamming shampoo bottles down and stomping my feet in the shower…throwing my fit. After I thought about it a little longer and rinsed some of my attitude down the drain, I did decide to go to that church. I obeyed, but it was a reluctant obedience. I was going, but I was not going to be happy about it.

It wasn't that I didn't like this church—I loved it. But it was out of the comfort zone that I had created and it started fifteen minutes earlier than I was used to. God didn't tell me about this change in plans until I was in the shower, so now I was running late. This was inconvenient and with the time crunch to get there, I would not have as much time to get ready. Vanity was on the line. I would have agreed to this plan more readily if God had given me more time to primp: that's the ugly truth.

Anyhow, I made it to church, found my seat, and crossed my arms. Something good better happen here! "You better have a good reason for dragging me to this church and making me rush!" What a great attitude to have in church, but at least I was there, right? Hadn't I done what God asked me to do? Wasn't I being obedient? Maybe technically, but certainly not in my heart.

Chip On My Shoulder

That chip on my shoulder was about to get knocked off in God's gentle way. The music was loud, but good. I was just not feeling in the mood to worship. Why should I give God glory when He was in debt to me? In my grief economy, God still owed me. So I pouted in the corner, right there in the second row. It can be done: you can be right smack-dab in the middle of something physically and your heart can be a million miles away. But God was about to close the gap.

A young woman I had never seen before stepped up to the microphone. This long-haired man with a lone guitar strummed and picked away at my stubborn pride and then this young woman sang. And when I say sang, I mean she SANG! Her voice was heavy and raspy and she seemed to be singing right through me as she emptied herself out to God. This woman could SING. Her voice seemed to echo my own heart's cry and as it reverberated back to me, I was finally able to hear God's mercy. Tears filled my eyes. What a beautiful song! What a glorious moment!

Heart Melt

The tall man with the smooth guitar and the woman with the haunting voice continued to warm my ice-cold, demanding, bargaining heart. It melted slowly out of my eyes as tears streamed down. As she emptied herself, healing came flooding into me. God was bringing healing in His own way and His own time and my stubborn heart had almost missed it.

The air was full of electricity as this duo strummed on. Beautiful. Powerful. Transcendent. It was as if they could tune into heaven's frequency and transmit its sounds to our earthly ears. The song dove deep and then rang out triumphantly with heavy pauses in between. And in that church, I realized that God had my best interests at heart. He knew where I needed to be on that morning and what I needed to hear to heal.

I didn't have to barter with God; I didn't have to be demanding. God was not out to rip me off or scam me. God loved me. He had just sung His love song over me. He wanted me to have every opportunity to get what I needed. And even though I wanted God to grant me my wishes like a good genie should, He would prove me wrong on two accounts.

First, God was no genie in a bottle and He would not be told what to do. I was not in charge, He was; and if I wanted Him to do what I said…well, that would not work. I had better get rid of the chip on my shoulder or bow my head and bend my knee, because He is God. And even though I am His child, it was time for me to quit throwing tantrums and hissy fits and realize a thing

117

or two. God loved me enough to put me in my proper place that day, and I will never forget it.

And second, God doesn't want to haggle with me, He wants to heal me. I could continue to threaten and demand that God give me what I wanted, or I could trust God to give me what I needed. It was a defining moment. Would I drop my demands and trust Him to heal me, or harden my heart and only meet God on my terms? A choice had to be made.

As demanding as I had been of God, He was not demanding of me. I had freedom to choose whatever I would do. He gave me the option to choose or refuse. I could trust Him to know what I needed even more than I knew myself, or I could refuse to obey Him and do things on my own. What would I choose, my way or the highway? God's ways are higher than our ways.

Job

I am reminded of Job in the Old Testament. Job's is a story of epic loss and severe trial. In one day Job lost his whole family, his money, and his health. He lost everything except his wife. His children were all dead, his riches evaporated, and he was covered in sores. Job basically said that the Lord gives and the Lord takes; Job still chose to bless the name of the Lord. I can't imagine such grief. How was Job able to face such tremendous loss and still say in his heart, "Blessed be the name of the Lord"?

Well, it wasn't because Job got good advice from his wife. At one point she encouraged Job to curse God and die—just end it all.

End the suffering, heartache, and loss by ending his life. Maybe you have considered this yourself. I hope you will be encouraged by the end of this story. Hang on.

Job's friends were no help, either. In essence, they told Job that he must have done something wrong for this entire calamity to fall on him. Maybe you are wrestling with guilt over the loss you have experienced. Perhaps you are feeling that somehow this is entirely your fault. You believe your sin has brought this on. You feel you deserve it. Job's friends were wrong: Job had not done anything to incur these losses. The Lord gives and the Lord takes. We don't understand why things happen the way they do. Only God knows.

Job chose not to curse God as his wife had suggested, and he did not take responsibility for causing the tragedy as his friends had suggested. Job did what I did and what you may be doing: He asked God. God pretty much refused to haggle with Job. God gently put Job in his place by asking Job who he was to question God. This is my interpretation of what God told Job: "Did you roll out the ocean and tell it where to stop? Did you lay out the stars in the sky and name them one by one? You will never understand all that I have done for you and all that I place into order everyday for you. Do not tell Me that I was out of order when these things happened to you. Just because you don't like what has happened to you does not give you the right to judge Me. I am not asking for your approval. Do not question My love in light of your circumstances. Trust Me. I am not punishing you. In this world, you will have trouble.

119

You can rail against Me or you can collapse into Me, but don't tell Me that I don't love you—I do. I am here for you. I want to help you."

Character vs. Circumstances

Job trusts God's character in spite of his circumstances. Job goes through grief, just like we all do. He gets mad and questions God. He gets sad and wails and weeps. He takes his grief to God and haggles with Him for answers. And in the end, Job finds healing.

I have been particularly encouraged by Job's story because he wrestles openly with all the stages of grief. Job reminds me to trust God's character in spite of my circumstances.

And I love the ending of this story: because Job trusts God through the trial, Job is doubly blessed. Because Job continues to say, "Blessed be the name of the Lord," even when his whole world is falling apart, God blesses Job. Job blessed God and God blessed Job. Around our house we call this phenomenon "2X blessed."

Hang on for the blessing. I look at it this way: God knows what we really need. He knows that our deepest need is to know that He is good when life is bad. We need to know that whatever happens to us in this life, God will get us through it. God wants me to know that He can give me new life even in the face of death. And He wants you to know it, too. That is what I call a happy ending.

Tired of Bargaining?

Bargaining with God and trying to manipulate God into giving you what you want is natural. But it is only a stage of grief, so we don't want to stay in the bargaining phase. We want to move on into the acceptance phase of grief. Acceptance is the final phase of grieving, so we are almost home.

Let's unlock the bargaining. Get out your keys:
D=Dare to Dream
R=Remove the Stinger
E=Embrace Awkward
A=Ask for Help

The Key to Unlock Bargaining: Ask for Help

In order to neutralize the bargaining phase, we need to ask for help. Instead of haggling with God or harassing others to get what we want, we just need to use our manners and ask politely. Asking for help is the key to unlocking the grip of grief in the bargaining phase.

I would like to break this "asking for help" down into two categories: asking for spiritual help and asking others for help.

Asking for Spiritual Help

We have talked about praying to God before in this book. I want to specify what I mean by asking God for help to neutralize the bargaining phase. It is simply this: ask God to help, and listen for His guidance and answers. The Psalms are full of

121

David's cries for help to God. Read through the Psalms for examples of how to ask for help from God. David was open and honest with God about the struggles he was facing. David did not hold back his sadness, anger, fear, and he even did some bargaining. Then, David asked God for what he needed. In the process of asking God for help, David was also reminded of the goodness of God, His faithfulness, His great love, His mighty strength, and His power to prevail.

Asking God for help puts us in the position of dependence on His power, and allows our weakness to be a platform for God to be strong in us. God is able to guide us and lead us and strengthen us; we need help. God is our true help. God helps us when we can't help ourselves. God helps us when others don't know how to help us.

The first and primary place to ask for spiritual help is from God himself. Remember, Jesus died for us, so that means God's son was killed. God Himself became a griever: He grieved the death of His only son and it was a violent, horrible death. God knows firsthand what it feels like to have someone you love die. God has grieved—He knows your pain.

But, also, God raised Jesus from the dead, so God has the power to overcome death. God can help you to overcome the power of death in your own life. He is capable and He is available. Ask God to help you put His power into play in your own grief. God has been where you are now and He wants to heal you. Submit to His authority over death and watch Him bring new life into your heart.

A well known verse in the Bible is "Jesus wept." Jesus wept, because one of his friends died.

Lazarus was a close friend and after his death, Jesus visited Mary and Martha, Lazarus's sisters. Jesus became overwhelmed with the grief of the sisters. One sister was mad. She must have been in the anger phase as she yelled at Jesus. "If you had been here, my brother wouldn't have died."

Jesus cried for the sisters' pain. He wept with them and for them. I can see Jesus determining, even more than ever, to put an end to death, once and for all. Death makes us mad; death makes us sad. Jesus was a griever, just like you are. He knows how you feel. Do not miss the opportunity for Jesus to weep with you in your grief.

Jesus was with Mary and Martha in their grief. Sometimes the best thing that someone can do for you is to just be with you in your sadness. After the memorial for Mike, a small group of grievers gathered at our house. My mom was not sure what to do to help me. I remember asking her to just sit on the couch next to me and hold my hand. She wanted to do more, but I assured her that this would help me most of all. So she sat with me and held my hand. It was beautiful.

Comforter

Jesus wants to comfort you and although He can't be with you like He was with Mary and Martha, He is with you in spirit. When Jesus was getting ready to leave Earth, he told his disciples that he would not leave them as orphans: He would send the Comforter.

Jesus assured His followers that even though He was going to the Father, He would not leave them fatherless. He even went as far as to say it was better for Him to go, so that the Comforter could take His place. What could be better than Jesus? The Spirit is given to those who believe in Jesus. The Helper is here to help us.

Comforter, Helper, and Spirit are all names for the presence of God in your life.

Who better to ask for comfort than the Comforter? Who better to ask for help than the Helper? When Jesus went to heaven, He sent His Spirit to be with us on Earth. If you have never thought much about the Holy Spirit, now is the time. The Spirit has become such a comfort to me in my grief. The Helper has been more help to me than any other person from whom I've received support.

If this Spirit thing is all new to you, don't let it scare you. Basically, God is giving you a piece of Himself to carry in your heart. Spirit is a reminder that God is with you. Spirit is a voice to guide you and a hand to help you. There is nothing scary or freaky—Spirit is just a gift from heaven for your heart.

When I sit quietly and ask for guidance from the Father, what I need to know more than anything is that He is with me. The best help He can give me is His Presence. Just like my mom sitting quietly with me on the couch holding my hand, God is with you in Spirit.

As I am writing this section of the book, my daughter Faith is getting ready to go on a first date with a new guy. She is nervous and even though I will not be with her physically tonight, she knows that I go with her in spirit.

Just knowing that I am with her calms her down and makes her feel more confident.

God is with you in Spirit. The Spirit is with you. Allow this presence to calm your nerves and make you feel more confident. You are not going through this life on your own - even if you feel alone - because God is with you. Take comfort and courage in the fact that God goes with you wherever you go.

We need spiritual help, but we also need a little help from other people.

Monkey Buddies

Monkey Buddies...what are they? And what do they have to do with grieving? There was a study done on monkeys: a stress test. That's right...a monkey stress test! I am not making this up. It went something like this...

A number of monkeys were put into individual cages and then introduced to stress, such as loud noises and flashing lights. The monkeys started freaking out! They were some STRESSED MONKEYS! Now, I don't know how they determine a monkey's stress level - I am not sure I want to know that part of the story! They tested the stress level of the monkeys and then repeated the test, only this time they changed one single factor in this fascinating test.

This time around, some of the monkeys were left alone in their cages and some of the monkeys were given a buddy to be in the cage with them. Their buddy was another monkey or a stuffed animal. The test was duplicated with the same loud noises and flashing lights. The exact same stressors were introduced as before, but this time the test results changed.

125

Do you know what they found? I am sure you are hanging on the edge of your seat, so I will tell you.

The monkeys who had a buddy in their cage with them were 50% LESS STRESSED than the monkeys who were left alone in their cage.

Can the mere presence of a buddy really CUT STRESS IN HALF? I am fascinated by the idea that going through stress ALONE was twice as hard as going through the same stress with a buddy. If monkeys need buddies, what about humans? Humans are subject to stress daily. Our nerves are tested by life every single day as grievers. Hopefully you are not in a cage, but wouldn't it make sense that if monkeys need buddies, maybe we do, too?

Bottom line: We need each other...as monkeys and as humans. This study just goes to confirm my long-standing belief that everybody needs a buddy. Evidently, monkeys do, too.

Asking for Help from Others

When your loved one dies, probably one of the things you will hear most from friends and family is, "If you need anything, you just let me know." I believe these people are being honest with you. They care for you and what you are going through. They want to help in any way that they can.

In the initial stages of grief, you may be overwhelmed with everything there is to do to rebuild your life. Meals, cards, and flowers are loving gestures sent to help you cope during those first few weeks. Friends and family want to know how they can be there for you, so don't be afraid to ask for what you need.

Most of your supporters would like to help, but may not know how. This is where it is vital for you to think of things they can do for you and ask them. I will give you some examples of how I asked for help and how friends and family were glad to oblige.

Run Like Mike

Right away neighbors and friends decided that one of the things they wanted to do to celebrate Mike was to host a run at a local park on the morning of his memorial. Mike was a runner and this seemed like a perfect way to celebrate him. I was already so busy planning the memorial - I was not sure I could pull this off as well.

I asked my two neighbors to be in charge of the event, and they were happy to do it. Stacy and Libby did it all: they arranged for the park pavilion to be reserved, coordinated with others who wanted to help, and mapped out the course. One of our friends volunteered to set up his sound system and play the music on Mike's iPod that he listened during his runs. There were yellow balloons, loud music, and everything to make the event joyful. All I did was order some bright yellow headbands with the words RUN LIKE MIKE written across them and show up.

The morning of the memorial run was beautiful and everyone was full of smiles and hugs, just like Mike would have wanted it. Friends had gladly volunteered to make this morning truly memorable. There was an article in the

127

newspaper in honor of Mike and the RUN LIKE MIKE event. One of Faith's friends had even posted signs along the course with scriptures to encourage the runners. It was perfect. They honored Mike and they helped me by doing it all on their own.

Bodyguards

Another example of friends stepping in to help me out happened the first week that Mike died. You see, Mike died on a Tuesday night and that coming Friday was Homecoming for our school. Abbi was a senior and Faith was a sophomore and I didn't want them to miss the homecoming game. I was also aware that this would be a hard game for me to go to without Mike. I needed backup, so I called my friends Rachel and Cheryl and asked if they would escort me to the game. I knew that without them, this outing would require more strength than I had as a freshly grieving widow. It would be my first time in a public place following his death just three nights prior. I knew I could count on my two bodyguards to stand with me and help me navigate the huge crowd at the football game.

These two friends picked me up at my house and drove me to the game. They stuck by me the whole time. They gave me support at a time when I truly needed it and they were happy to do it.

After many hugs and greetings from adults and students, the game was half over. I was exhausted and ready to go home. My two friends drove me home and dropped me off with hugs and kisses.

I will never forget their presence with me when I really needed it. I am so glad I asked for their help.

Driving Lessons

When Mike died, Faith did not have her license to drive yet. She did have her temporary license, which meant that she could drive if she had a licensed driver with her. I will be honest with you, I did not have the steady nerves needed to ride with an inexperienced driver. My nerves were already shot dealing with the sudden death of my husband and all the mountains of paperwork and raw emotions. I was not ready to teach her how to drive, but she was ready to learn.

Mike's best friend, Bryan, who is also my brother-in-law, was called in to help out. Bryan took Faith to the school parking lot and spent two hours with her teaching her to drive. Faith was able to work out some of the bugs of being a new driver and could practice in an open area. Bryan coached her in applying the brakes, pulling in and out of parking spaces, and holding the wheel steady. They even went for ice cream before returning home.

Bryan stepped up to the plate and covered me early on, so that Faith could begin learning to drive. He took her out several times so that she learned how to actually drive on the road. He was patient and direct and encouraging to this new driver. He was also extremely helpful to me by doing what I could not yet do. It was not too long till I was able to take over the driving lessons, but I am thankful for Bryan's willingness to help me when I really needed it.

Closet Cleaning

One of the hardest jobs for me to do, emotionally, was to clean out Mike's clothes from my closet. I put it off for the longest time, but it was hard to walk into my closet and still see his clothes hanging there. It made me miss him more and was actually hurting my heart instead of healing it. I knew I needed to do it, but who could help me with this?

Then I thought of my sister-in-law, Melissa. She has done professional cleaning and organizing for years—she was perfect. Not only was she a professional, but I knew she would be able to help me emotionally with this task. She is a small woman, but she is strong, both physically and emotionally. So, I asked Melissa if she would help me clean out Mike's clothes and we set a date for her to come down and help me.

On the morning she showed up, we hugged and cried and sorted through shirts, jeans, and uniforms. We made three piles: things to keep, things to give away, and things I was not sure what to do with yet. We moved the things we were keeping out of my closet and downstairs to a spare bedroom closet.

Then, she helped me bag up the things to give away and we put them in her car. The items I was uncertain about were bagged and put in storage to be dealt with later. It was a hard day, but I was so thankful for her willingness to help me do what I could not bear to do by myself.

Your List

Look through the myriad of things that need to be done and see which ones others can help you with. Make a list of things that need to be done, and ask your friends and family which tasks they are able to do. Most likely they will be able to help in some way, and be glad to do it. You will be glad they did, too.

Do you need someone to:

- Take out the trash?
- Pick up prescriptions?
- Drop off groceries?
- Do yard work?
- Clean out the fridge?
- Repair items around the house?
- Clean the house?
- Babysit?
- Teach you to pay bills, do taxes, or other bookkeeping tasks?
- Drive you to run errands?
- Take you to coffee?
- Do car maintenance?
- Take you to exercise?
- Do your laundry?

If friends and family want to help, but you're overwhelmed and don't know how to respond, please see Chapter 7: Dear DREAM Team.

Double Grief

Grief is complicated enough on its own, but I have found that mine was intensified by one thing. There was a simple element that took my pain

131

and multiplied it greatly. I write about it now as my strongest warning to you. It is something that, even though I had heard about it and even experienced it to a certain degree before in my life, it still rocked me. I would even go as far as to say that it caused me to "double grieve."

What could possibly have the ability to make my misery double in size? What one factor could compound the pain so severely that I would almost break? It was the judgments of people who I thought, and hoped, would be compassionate. It was the criticism of family or friends: the harsh and disapproving questions and the cold, demeaning, condemning comments that almost broke me.

My experience with friends and family during this process was mostly supportive, understanding, and compassionate, and I thank God for that. But, there were a few pivotal times when I received such a lack of grace that I was brought to my emotional end and experienced new grief on top of my original grieving. My warning to the griever is to help you know that this kind of criticism does happen, so that you are not blindsided by it when it does. This is a helpful reminder to guard your heart from those who are critical. Prepare yourself for a variety of reactions from people watching you grieve.

Decorating Dilemma

My husband died while he was sitting in the car; his heart just stopped. Suddenly my world twisted and changed right before my eyes. He was dead in the driveway. Now I had two daughters looking at me in shock. What do we do? How do we go on? This is our home. This is our house. This is where we have lived for ten years as a family. In the kitchen there are four chairs around the table, but now there are only three of us. In my walk-in closet, there is one side of Mike's clothes and one side of mine. In our master bedroom is a huge king sized bed and no more "king," no more "master."

I have been an interior decorator for 25 years and I know the power of the home environment. It is a sacred space for family. Now our home was hurting, we were hurting. I needed the house to help us heal. Later that fall, after I had been sleeping on the couch for two months, not able to rest in my own bedroom, I decided to redecorate my bedroom as a Christmas gift to myself. I had to replace the king bed with a queen—it seemed only appropriate. I picked out a new, softer mattress and changed the color scheme to "spa" colors of beiges and creams, with soft blue accents for the new bedroom. I was trying to create a calm and relaxing space for my frayed nerves to heal and rest.

I hired a friend to paint the walls and hang the curtains, but the rest of the work I did by myself. I started from scratch with new lamps, new bedding, new art, and a new bed.

It was therapeutic for me and the end product was amazingly tranquil. I slept like a baby for the first time in months. It was the best gift I could have received during that first hard Christmas season without my husband. My new bedroom was a place to rest, heal, grieve, and learn to live without him. It was what I needed to do to heal.

133

Now, I have talked to other widows who have not changed a thing in their bedroom. Everything is exactly as it was before the death of their husband. They have the same sheets, same lamps, and same pictures on the wall. This provides them with what they need for comfort and stability during so much loss. It is how they choose to heal.

No Right or Wrong

In matters of decorating, there is no wrong or right here. There is no rule that says you must not change the bedroom or you must change the bedroom. There is room for personal preference. There are choices we as grievers make in the healing process that, frankly, are nobody else's concern. I did receive both approval and disapproval from friends and family on the bedroom renovation. Obviously the girls understood this need for change and supported me in it, but I also had people who thought they could sit in a seat of judgment and condemn my choice to redecorate the master bedroom. Funny thing is, these people rarely share their comments or concerns to you directly; they're usually whispered to another friend or family member. "Did you hear that Kristi redecorated the bedroom? I don't think she should have done that. I think she will regret that later. I would never do that."

Sleeping Single in a Double Bed

Well, again to you critical "bystanders," it is not your call to make. You are not the one sleeping single in a double bed. And if you are, that is your choice. You are free to make your own choices, and I am free to make my own decisions about what will help me heal. Within the next year, I went ahead and redecorated the whole house. His office now became my office. The airplane pictures were replaced by a large artwork of a woman standing tall and proud and strong: she was my inspiration piece. Our walk in closet became a dressing area for me with feminine art, a chandelier, and soft, fuzzy carpet. The rectangular kitchen table with four chairs was replaced by three chairs and a round table, making it less obvious that someone was missing at the table. We allowed ourselves to be a family of three now. As we redefined our space, we also realigned our home around the reality of our beautiful family of three women.

To me this was also a way to honor my husband and our family of four. Because we had built this house together, we decided to stay in this house. But it also was a way to honor our newly established family of three women. I still feel the love and life that my husband and the girl's father invested into this place and more importantly into us as people. But our house has changed to reflect the change in our family.

REMINDER: There is freedom to choose what works for you and your direct family. Friends and extended family would do well to allow you grace and breathing space. As long as no emotional or physical harm is done to anyone else, there should be lots of room for personal choice and healing options.

135

Stay or Move

Even though Mike died here on our property, it was still our choice to stay here. We figured the years of life, love, and laughter invested here were worth more than a few moments of shock, grief, and loss in the driveway. Now, to you on the outside, you might be saying, "I could never live there. I would have to move. I could never go back to that house again." First of all, I hope you never have to make that call. And secondly, if you do have to decide whether to sell or stay, or redecorate versus leave things as they are, know there is no wrong answer. You do what you need to do to continue healing. Honor yourself without dishonoring others, and you are free to choose what fits your life. I will not be judging you and hopefully other friends and family members won't either. But if you do feel judged, just remember this warning from today and don't let their critical spirits take your spirit down. I encourage you; I give you the courage to make your own choices. Receive courage, because it is needed more than ever before.

BE COURAGEOUS!

People-Pleasing

In these few examples of the choices I made, to stay in our home and to redecorate, I hope it has been made obvious to you that there were people who approved and disapproved of my choices. TRUTH: there is no way to please everyone! If you have ever struggled with people-pleasing (and I think we all have) you will have to deal with that demon in order to heal; otherwise you will make yourself more miserable. And who needs more misery? Not me! And certainly not you!

Personal Choice

Grieving is a very personal process. What you need to do to heal will not look the same as what I require to heal. This is why I think it is important for me to give you permission to honor yourself. Not that you need my permission, but maybe you need to give yourself permission to honor yourself. It may sound strange to give yourself permission to be yourself, but I think it may be more vital to the healing process than you think.

Sometimes, amid all the loss, you can kind of lose yourself for awhile. Finding yourself again requires holding on to the parts of you that cannot ever be lost and rebuilding with those parts.

Things like your values, your personality, and your character cannot be taken away from you by any loss suffered. But things like your personal preferences, your style, and your individual goals can certainly be affected by loss. Who you were before the loss will not be exactly who you are after the loss.

It's important to be careful who you choose to have beside you in the grief process. Not to be rude, but be selective about who you spend your time with. You are in a delicate transition and you need people who can understand and support you through it. Give yourself permission to say yes and no to those who seek to spend time with you.

Not everyone will know how to navigate these rough waters with you. You are changing and not everyone will like the change.

Who Am I Now?

I believe that in the long run, "losing yourself" is only temporary. We may get thrown by the loss or the longing and have to re-adjust, but ultimately God has the ability to help us rise above the grief, be transformed by it, and come out stronger on the other side. If I didn't believe this, I would have given up long ago. If you didn't believe this, you would not be reading this book.

We are all looking for the same thing: the ability to take whatever this world brings and not get bitter, but get better. It's the goal of every human on the planet. How do we grieve and lose and yet ultimately, eventually, heal? How do we take the things that happen to us and use them to grow us and not limit us? How can we help our family or friends struggle through and make it to a higher place? How do we come to terms with longing for more, yet living with less.

Redefining yourself after the devastation is crucial. Remember who you were. Be honest with who you are now. Allow yourself to be transformed by the pain, to become a more compassionate and caring person. Give yourself grace to figure out who exactly you are going to be when the healing is complete. You are making great strides toward becoming whole again. You are grieving gracefully.

A Child's Prayer

Grieving is like praying; with two hands folded together in a simple pose, we ask for divine guidance. One hand holds the pain, the loss, the longing, the uncertainty, the brokenness, the fear, the questions, the tears, and the emptiness. The other holds the healing, the possibilities, the contentment, the hope, the joy, the faith, the answers, the smiles, and the fullness. It is in the bringing together of the hands that praying leads to new life. All of our sadness becomes entwined with His sacred wholeness and we are transformed. One hand of sorrow is wrapped in the other hand of unquenchable joy and we find peace.

Grieving is like a child's prayer. As God's dearly loved children, we bring our grief to our Father. We ask Him to heal our hearts.

It is in the bringing together of the two extremes, the left hand and the right hand, where death and life combine. The fist of grief must open to the hand of healing. Fingers of fear mingle with fingers of faith and we become whole. Hands folded together, hearts open to healing. God is invited into our presence. Suddenly, past and present collide in a fireworks display and we begin to see what was, what is, and what can be.

Prayer for Asking for Help

Dear God, we beg for You to help us through this grief. We feel torn apart and scattered by the severe pain of separation from our loved ones. We are powerless to illuminate the darkness of death. We feel abandoned and shredded by severe longing in our lives. We call on You, Father of Lights, to show us the way. Lead us through the valley of the shadow of death and fill the empty spaces in our hearts. Restore our souls. Reclaim our lives. We are hopeless without You.

As we fold our hands in holy surrender to Your goodness, bring together the pieces of our lives. Infuse Your presence into our pain. Be with us. Remind us of Your authority over death. Embrace us with Your love. Consume our fear and fill us with faith. In You, we are certain of life after death. We need new life.

Enfold Your hands around ours and enable us to be healed. We entrust our tomorrows to You today. Give us strength and courage to be honest with You, ourselves, and others about the dual realities we feel: hurt and hope, fear and faith, life and death. Combine these seemingly opposing forces into one grand Life Force. Be in us and with us. Deliver and sustain us. Draw near and stay with us. We need You.

Thank You for being our Creator and Re-Creator. Create in us what we cannot call forth on our own. Give us new life. Give us hope that never dies. Help us to know that You see us, You love us, and You will never leave us. God, we are dependent on You, and it is in that dependence that we are freed from the bondage of grief. We are free to feel and heal. Free to lose and love. Free to be free. In holy honor, we fold our hands and bow our heads to You. Through the power of Your Risen Son, raise us up to walk in newness of life. We ask all these things in Jesus's name. Amen.

Chapter 5

Move On: Lock In Acceptance

Acceptance is the much sought after trophy of grief; the Grand Prize of healing! This final stage of grief is defined by your ability to incorporate your loss or longing into your everyday life. Your whole existence is no longer focused on the past and what has or hasn't happened to you. You are now able to focus on the present and what has happened in you, and look forward to the future and what will happen through you.

You have worked hard to arrive here. You have walked through the deep valley and have now reached the height of healing. You are able to deal with the reality of what was, be present with what is, and look forward to what can be. Yesterday, today, and tomorrow co-exist in your mind.

You have decided that when your world changed, you would change with it. You have quit fighting the change and running from the results of the change and steadfastly determined to make the best of it. Not able to change the past, you have made peace with it. Being present in today, you have acknowledged the power of loving and being fully alive. Acceptance is allowing what has transpired to affect you, but not limit your ability to grow from it. Acceptance acknowledges that you are limitless.

Grace Place

You have weathered the seasons of grief and stand in the grace of this new place. You are stronger for what you have endured, but not hardened by it. You have deeper compassion and a renewed passion for living out the remainder of your days with purpose. You have been through hard times, but you are not hardened. You are softened and able to be gentle to yourself and those around you. You are able to bend without breaking.

Acceptance brings the five graces of grief full circle. You have been in denial, anger, sadness, and even bargained with God to change what happened. You have processed the profound effects of not being able to be with your loved ones and you have decided to carry them in your heart instead. You have wrestled with your longings and come to peaceful terms with them. Your heart has grown and expanded from the exercise of grieving and instead of being unable to live or love, you have an increased capacity to live and love.

Grief has not shut you down, but opened you up. You love more freely and are more able to give and receive love.

You know when someone grieves the greatest thing that lasts is the love. Love is eternal; loss does not destroy love and longing cannot take our chance for love away...love remains. There is nothing in all creation worth more than living and loving. So, you carry on with your head held high, your eyes full of grace, and your heart full of gratitude. You have been purified by grief. It has not poisoned your ability to live, but ever increased your capacity to love. You have reached the place of acceptance.

Move On: Locking In Acceptance

Moving on is about accepting what is. I am not suggesting that you need to be happy about what has happened, but I am asking you to let it be. To make peace with the pain. To allow the heartache to heal. To quit fighting against reality. One little step at a time. One breath at a time. One minute at a time. Moving on is not about abandoning our dreams or forgetting our loved ones. Moving on is simply doing the next thing it takes to live.

I can hear you asking me, "How does someone accept divorce after a long drawn out battle? How would you suggest for someone to come to a point of acceptance when their hair is falling out and scars are crisscrossing their chest? How would you move on if your daughter committed suicide?" These are hard questions so I will answer them softly. Before I can answer your first round of questions you start with the second round. "Are you telling me to move on without my loved one? To move on without having what I long for?" The answer is yes. I am asking you to move on, but probably not in the way you are picturing. Let me give you an example.

A local father was visibly angry with me when he arrived at this point in the book. He was outraged at my seemingly insensitive directive to move on. "Now, wait a minute here little missy. Move on?! I will never move on without my daughter! How dare you tell me to move on! She was my life. I can't go on without her. When I saw that last chapter in your book, I didn't even read it. I just put the book down. Move on!?"

I could see the pain in his eyes? It had been less than a year since his small daughter had died in a tragic car accident. I didn't want to do anything but validate his anger. It can be excruciating to move on after someone has died. For this devoted father moving on was not about forgetting what had happened to his little girl or dishonoring her memory. Moving on for him would be to one day be able to get in a car and drive again or someday buckle his other daughters into their car seats. Maybe for him moving on would be to be able to sit at a stop sign and keep breathing. In and out. Breathing.

With some clarification I came to find out these were things that he had already done. He was already moving on. He just didn't realize it. He thought moving on would require him to forget her. What I mean when I say Move On is not to forget your loved ones. First of all, we can't forget them, and secondly, we don't want to forget them. No. Moving on is not about forgetting where we were, whom we once loved, what we once had, or what we so desperately long for. Especially in this case, moving on was not to forget his daughter's memory – it was a way to honor her memory.

Moving on will be hard, but it should be do-able. It will require courage, but you will be able to manage it. Moving on happens over time and is a process. Remember: the overall goal of moving on is to lock in acceptance. The key to locking in acceptance is to Move On.

Moving on is meant to be a verb; an action word. In order to lock in acceptance you will be required to do something. This is not so much a mental exercise as it is a physical activity. Acceptance can happen on an emotional or mental level. But I think in order to make it stick, to make it solid, to LOCK IN the acceptance you will need to do something. What will you need to do? It's different for each situation, but here are a few possibilities of what moving on can look like.

- Eat at the dinner table alone
- Move from sleeping on the couch back into your bedroom
- Write a letter of thanks to your mother
- Send a card or text to your estranged father
- Smile politely at your new boss (he or she may wonder what you are up to)
- Go on a blind date
- Babysit your friend's kids for an evening
- Work on forgiving the drunk driver
- Register for that exercise class you've been meaning to take
- Sit by someone new at church
- Dance in your living room
- Send out your updated resume
- Pray for your ex-spouse
- Celebrate your co-worker's promotion
- Downsize to a smaller house or apartment
- Phone an old friend
- Hug someone

145

- Give some grace…especially to yourself
- Buy some new lingerie just for fun
- Go to a movie with your teenager
- Sing in the shower
- Buy some ice-cream for an elderly neighbor
- Make someone's favorite meal
- Look a homeless person in the eyes
- Say thank you to your spouse

Healing

Now that you have reached this sacred place of healing it is OK to Move On. Live and love out of the depth of your heart. Love unconditionally. Be brave. Stand tall. Be thankful for the journey. Help those you know who encounter death to learn to love again and help those who get entangled in longing to learn to live again. Shine light on the path for them. Tell them about the stepping stones to wholeness and be sure to remind them of the gifts you have received along the way. They may be inspired by the light in your eyes to have hope—hope is essential.

Point friends to the Life-Giver and tell them of His kindness and unfailing mercy. Bring God your thanks for His presence in your life. Praise God for the power to face loss and longing with courage, which is a miracle in and of itself. Live, love, and laugh, because God has turned your deep sorrow into dancing. Dare to dream and dare to dance and dare to fully live. I dare you.

Defining Moment

I will share another true "Kristi Smith story" that was a defining moment in my life. As I sat at a wedding reception last fall, the DJ announced, "I need all the single ladies out on the dance floor. In a few minutes, the bride will be throwing the bouquet. We ask all you single ladies to make your way out onto the dance floor at this time." This was an announcement I had heard multiple times throughout my life; there was nothing unusual there. What made this time stand out for me was that, after almost 25 years of marriage, this time the DJ was talking to me.

It was surreal. The music started playing. You might know the song…"All the single ladies, all the single ladies, all the single ladies…" You can't hear me singing right now and that is probably a good thing, because I am sure I am butchering the song, but all of the sudden I realized this song was calling me out onto the dance floor. I was now a "single lady." Exactly one year prior to this young bride's wedding day, I had "celebrated" my husband's birthday for the first time without him. Now on this second birthday after his death, I found myself for the first time at a wedding as a widow. Widow is just another word for "suddenly single." Sitting there at the reception with the music pounding in my ears and my heart pounding even louder, I realized I had a choice to make. Would I stay seated and ignore the call? Or would I answer the call and join the other single ladies on the dance floor? It was a defining moment.

147

Answer the Call

Next thing I knew, my feet were walking toward the sound of the music and all these 20-something women soon surround me. Here I was a "seasoned woman" in her…let's just say mid to late 40's…all right…late 40's…okay, fine…I was 49! And I stood in the middle of a swarm of girls with my two daughters on either side of me. We were completely encircled by all their young friends who were all laughing and vying for positions behind the bride. Some of the girls noticed me and out of their love for me helped move me to center point behind the quarterback. This only seemed to make an awkward situation for me somehow more uncomfortable.

The bride hiked the ball—I mean the bouquet—and I saw this mass of multihued flowers coming straight for my face. Instinct kicked in and all of the sudden I was wrestling some girl for the prized bouquet. Maybe it was because I am a "seasoned woman" or maybe because she saw the look of terror in my eyes, but my daughter released her grip on the flowers and let her mama have that moment of glory (not really sure what all happened, it happened so fast!). I then proceeded to do some kind of embarrassing dance like a running back in the end zone followed by a quick victory lap around the dance floor with my head held high and the fragrant spoils of this single-lady contest lifted higher in the air for all to see. The thrill of victory. The agony of defeat.

That evening, memories were made. My daughters and I laughed and danced for hours and it was a pivotal night for all of us. Looking back, I realize that it was at that wedding that I started to allow God to turn my sorrow into dancing…literally. Life is filled with twists and turns and hills and valleys. All along the path we are given opportunities to sit idly by or to get out onto the dance floor. We can either ignore the call or dance the night away. And like the country song says, "I hope you dance." This is your official invitation to Move On. Dare to dance. This might be your defining moment.

Grief is a Gift

An obscure thought comes to me this morning as I sit quietly on the deck, soaking in the sun, on this crisp fall day. When did this shift happen in my soul? It seems like yesterday I was caught up in the grief of death. Today, almost two years since my husband passed, a new awareness takes hold in my heart. It startles me awake to new possibilities. What if the grief of death is also the gift of life?

As I ponder this profound statement, my insides are illuminated as much as the sunshine is warming my outside. What if the pain of death and loss and sorrow is also a gift to bring about new life and prosperity and joy? Could the grave of darkness, despair, and sadness become the fertile ground that produces sacred seedlings of light, determination, and peace?

I receive it as truth: grief can be a gift and death can lead to new life. The honesty of these thoughts shoots through me like a bright dawn after a long night. This truth is unmistakably brilliant, clear, and transforming.

149

Fields of Grace

I am being taught a life lesson. Unlike a school lesson that can sometimes seem irrelevant to real-life issues, this life lesson is touching every part of me and seems to jump off the page and into my consciousness. I am presented with this question: if we plant grief, can grace grow? And if so, how? I don't pretend to know the intimacies of God's climate, but this I know for sure: Nothing is too hard for God.

When I take my pain and desperate pleas to God, can He grow them into fields of grace? Out of the ashes of destruction and broken dreams, can hope arise? I will be perfectly frank...we, as humans, do not have the ability to cultivate such crops. We do not have the resources or power to plant grief and grow grace. At first, this can sound like bad news, but it's not.

Brokenness into Beauty

If humans were expected to grow grace from grief, we would be crushed by the pressure of trying to do so. As a griever I am already broken in ways that leave me feeling helpless. Grief can be consuming and debilitating. Don't look to me to know how to transform brokenness into beauty; I am at a loss. If I expected that of myself, I would sink into total despair. When others look to me to know how to overcome the pangs of death, I find myself sliding deeper into the pit.

No, I am not capable of such mighty feats of awesomeness. And that is good news, because I don't have to pretend to know how to bring death to life. This confession does not leave me in hopelessness, however, because there is One who does have the power to trump death. He has done it before and He will do it again…and again…and again. He is LIFE. He is Creator. He is God. He reminds me not to become overwhelmed with grief. Come to "Grace." The Spirit refuses to allow death to be the final word. Come to "LIFE."

God wants us to bring Him our broken hearts; He longs to make us whole again. He has the power. He has the ability. He has the willingness. God delights to bring us healing. He wants nothing more than to enter our pain and take us to His heart. Like a father, God wraps us in His loving embrace. Like a mother, God wipes our tears and listens to our heart cries. Like a friend, God walks closely with us. But God is better than a father, a mother, and a friend. He is God, which means that He has the skills to transform our grief into grace and turn the grave into sacred ground.

Sacred Ground

My husband was cremated, so there is no official gravesite for him, but I still love to visit cemeteries occasionally. There is something about the sacredness of the ground and the tall trees and the marble markers that connects me to healing. Cemeteries are usually park-like and picturesque, with rolling hills of green grass and well-manicured settings. It is holy ground. For me, it is a quiet, peaceful place to contemplate and complain and find comfort. I look around me at the beautiful statues of angels standing guard and notice that crosses decorate many of the markers.

I pause to think about the Cross. Isn't the Cross the place where death died? Isn't the Cross where death was defeated? Jesus died on the Cross. He died for you and for me and for all people; past, present, and future. The Cross marks time forever, because even though it was a place of death, it does not stand for death now. That place of death became the symbol for life. God in His great love and awesome power raised Jesus from the dead. The Cross, which was the place of death, became the property of the living. Fear was eclipsed by faith and death gave way to life.

Crossroads

You may find yourself like me...at a CROSSroads. God is there at your crossroads, just like He was there at the Cross. He wants to replace our fears with newfound faith and force death to yield to new life. He can do this for us—God can do for us what we cannot do for ourselves. God is here at your crossroads now, just as powerfully as He was at the Cross.

Dying on the Cross, Jesus committed His spirit into God's hands. Jesus surrendered His body to death, but He committed his spirit to a higher authority than death. Just like Jesus did on the Cross, we are asked to commit our spirits to our Father God.

Ways to Remember
Your Loved One

On the one-year anniversary of Mike's death, the "death-iversay," I was trying to figure out what to do to honor the day. We had already celebrated Mike's life together with friends and family in some really beautiful ways throughout the year, so I was struggling with what to do corporately. I was moved by the Spirit to not do another big production, but to have people honor Mike individually. This is the list of activities that I recommended for friends and family to do to honor Mike. They are practices that Mike had modeled to us and by putting them into practice, we would remember his life and bring honor to his memory.

- Go for a run
- Take a hike into the woods
- Go for an airplane ride
- Chop wood
- Hug your kids really tight
- Kiss your wife a little longer than normal
- Encourage a Young Life leader
- Take a buddy out for a beer
- Help a complete stranger
- Stop and listen to your neighbor
- Lay right on the sand at the beach
- Volunteer at church
- Give courage to a family member
- Say "I love you" several times throughout the day

153

- Start that awkward conversation you have been needing to have
- Forgive someone for doing something that you thought ruined your life (it didn't)
- Give someone a second chance (even if it is yourself)
- Take a risk
- Think outside the box
- Greet the day with a sense of adventure
- Have really great sex
- Be honest with your faults
- Use your gifts
- Talk about your spiritual life
- Don't back down from a challenge
- Dance even if you are not a good dancer
- Pray out loud
- Be really proud of your family
- Be REAL
- Take a shower outside
- Build a great fire
- Drop in on your friends

You may want to make your own list of things you want to do to honor your loved one's memory. Remember that the most important thing to do, what will truly honor the dead, is to truly live. Grieve as long and as loud as it takes to heal and then get back to life. Live fully alive to each day that you are given. Life is a gift. Tear into it.

Mike's Journal

There are two of my late husband's belongings that are sacred to me. These are elements I will keep and treasure.

One is a leather bound journal that he started writing about a year and a half before he died. In this journal, Mike shared some of his deepest thoughts on the most important topics of life. This was to be a hand-written gift to the girls. His last shared thoughts are dear to my daughters and me. I keep the journal in a fire-safe box. Mike's journal is a treasure, especially because none of us knew Mike was going to die; not even Mike. The Spirit must have prompted him to record these writings.

Mike's Bible

The second possession of Michael's that is sacred to me is one of his Bibles. Mike had several Bibles throughout his lifetime and they are all special to me, but the one I hold dear is the one that he was reading in his final days here on Earth. The worn, brown leather cover, the yellow highlighted verses, and the handwritten comments are evidence of Mike wanting to connect to God, to hear from God, and to know the heart of God.

I remember one day in particular, after Mike had gone to heaven. I was reading through his Bible. I was hoping desperately to hear a word of encouragement from God and to feel closer to my beautiful, beloved husband. As I thumbed through the pages, I noticed the crinkle of the paper and how there were certain passages that the book

155

would automatically fall open to from frequent use. I opened to the page that had the silky, golden bookmark. The ribbon felt like it was holding a special place for me. I decided to study this section closely for anything to speak peace to me. If this page was marked, there must be something important for my heart to hear.

Book Marker

I began at the top of the left page and started to scan the headings at Luke 19:44. There were red letters, where Jesus spoke, and black letters, which gave the backdrop of His three-year ministry. First, I found the story of Jesus at the temple as He was removing the resident robbers. Greed had entered and He was literally driving it out. He was cleaning house. His house would be a safe place for people to gather. I had always wanted to buy an old church building, remodel it, and make it into a house of prayer. It would be a quiet sanctuary where weary souls could come bring their life questions and, in quietness, find the answers. There would be a prayer wall and lots of artwork and a fireside room where you could get a cup of coffee and settle down into a comfy chair to read one of the many books from the shelves. Maybe I was to make my house into a house of prayer...was this the message I was supposed to hear from God? I continued scanning further into Luke 20.

Business and Taxes and Marriage

Next, Jesus told of a business with bad management. I don't know much about business so I kept reading. Jesus continued talking about paying taxes to Caesar. I pay my taxes, so I am good there. Then there was a very interesting passage about there being no marriage in heaven. I don't know what to think about that. Maybe God was letting me know that Mike was complete in heaven. Maybe Mike wasn't feeling like he was missing his other half, like I was feeling. Maybe Mike was not sad or feeling alone, like I was feeling. So I pictured Mike whole and happy and that was a gift.

But the passage from this marked page that jumped out to me was in the far right column of the second page, entitled, "The Widow's Offering" (Luke 21:1-4)."Widow" was the word that caught my attention, because I was a widow now.

Widow was a strange title that was thrust upon me with no warning or invitation. So I read about this other widow and her offering.

The Widow

Jesus looked up and saw the rich putting their gifts into the offering box. He also saw a poor widow put in two small copper coins. Jesus told the others that she put in everything she had to live on. WOW! This was definitely a passage meant for me to learn from. I take time to mill this one over. I ask for guidance in interpreting the application to my life. Am I to give all I have to God? Am I to take all my money and give it to the church? What did this newly appointed widow need to learn from this ancient widow?

The old widow whispered to me, "TRUST. Trust God." The widow had given all that she had to live on. She was trusting God to sustain her financially, but also with her whole life, her very life. TRUST GOD…yes, I need to hear this from another widow. Her faith inspires me to remember God's faithfulness to me.

I continue searching the widow's story to learn more about her. Verse one says that Jesus was watching the people put their gifts into the treasury. He saw the rich giving their gifts, but he also saw the widow; she only put in two very small copper coins, ancient pennies called mites. Her power came from trusting what little she had to the Power. Her strength was not in the size of her gift, but in the size of her trust.

Jesus saw her small gift among the rich offerings and knew that the widow's heart had given all that she had to live on. This woman was claiming her dependence on God, her reliance on Him, and stating that her life was in His hands. She believed. BELIEVED! Do I believe that God can be my provider, my Sustainer? Can I empty myself out trusting that God will fill me up again.

Believers

"Believers" is an old-fashioned term that has new meaning to me. This widow was a Christian, but she was also a "believer." She believed enough to put her faith into action. If God didn't prove real then she would be left destitute, without hope. Maybe emptied pockets can lead to fuller hearts?

Her belief challenged me. Do I believe? Am I willing to trust God to be real? Do I rely on Him to be my hope? Do I allow myself to be emptied out, so that He can fill me with His fullness? Yes, this was the passage that had been unwittingly marked for me to contemplate. The Spirit had moved Mike to leave this page marked for me. These four verses about the widow are even highlighted in yellow and they are the only verses on these two pages that are highlighted.

Scared or Sacred?

Whether you are a widow or not, I think the principle is the same. Dependence on God is the safest place to be. It may be scary, but I have noticed there is just a slight difference in how we spell scared and sacred: they contain the same letters, only in a different order.

It is my prayer that as I enter the times or places where I am scared that I will allow God to make them sacred. I pray the same for you.

Mighty Mites

The widow's mites became the widow's might! This widow from two thousand years ago was speaking to me in my grief: "Kristi, trust God. Believe. Put it all in His hands." The ancient widow was telling me that Jesus is watching; He sees my sacrifice, and He receives my gifts. Jesus notices me in my situation and He honors me. Just like Jesus commented on the widow's faith to those who were with Him, He speaks up for me when I think no one notices. Jesus said the widow put in more than all the others. Her two mites were mightier in His economy than the rich people with their larger offerings. The widow speaks to me still, "Give what you have. Leverage your life. TRUST. BELIEVE. Let God be mighty in you."

Prayer for Moving On

Dear God, Thank You for guiding us through grief and into healing. We are reminded of Your Presence with us and eternally grateful for Your great love for us. Thank You for reaching for us in the depths of our despair and gently leading us to Your heart. Thank You for giving us the strength and courage to face the emotions of grieving and thank You for unlocking the grip of grief on our hearts. May we honor You with the rest of our lives by being brave and living free. Thank You for the gift of life and for the power over death that we can have in Jesus. Help us to DREAM. Keep us close to Your heart and give our hearts wings— may we soar high and love deeply. We ask all these things boldly in the name of Jesus. Amen.

Chapter 6
DREAM Again

As you will recall, the five keys are:

D=Dare to dream, the key to unlock Denial
R=Remove the stinger, the key to unlock Anger
E=Embrace awkward, the key to unlock Sadness
A=Ask for help, the key to unlock Bargaining
M=Move on, the key to lock in Acceptance

I have strategically used the letters of the word DREAM as an acronym for the five keys so they would be easy to remember. Grief takes time and practice. I want you to be able to recall the five stages of grief alongside the five keys so that you can use the DREAM process to provide deeper healing. This will make it easier to keep track of your progress and then be able to use the acronym to prompt you as needed. For example...Do I need to Embrace awkward or Remove the stinger? Well, it depends if I am feeling angry or sad? I am feeling angry...so I know that I need to Remove the stinger.

I have personally cycled through the stages of grief several times. Each time that I have circled back through them I have experienced deeper healing. You may find the same is true for you. I call it "DREAM Again"...keep on DREAMing and keep on healing. The goal of grieving is to bring healing. You may need to go back through these grief stages on a recurring basis throughout the years. Don't be alarmed by this repetition: with each cycle back through the DREAM steps, you will have more meaningful healing.

As you repeat the DREAM steps, you may be led to pause at certain stages and to give yourself more time to incorporate the healing. You may walk through several steps with good cadence, but then get stuck on one step for a longer time.

Your experience will be customized to your grief. You may find that you breeze through all the steps the first time, but get caught up on one of them the second time through. You may slide through several steps in a row and then grind to a halt on one. Or, you may do the steps out of order. There is no rhyme or reason for how we grieve, so just trust yourself to grieve the way you need to heal. There is no exact order to the DREAM process, so don't be surprised if the steps change order. Sadness may come before anger one time through, but then reverse the next time.

The first time through the five stages of grief was the hardest for me, because I was learning so much and hurting so profoundly. The second time through the steps, I knew more what to expect with each stage, but I was still surprised by my progress. I was having a hard time being honest with my anger; processing my anger took longer than I expected.

I think that women tend to have a harder time with the anger stage and men tend to have a harder time with the sadness stage. This is a broad generalization, so don't be offended if you don't fit into these categories. Remember, grief is personal.

Repeat this five-step process as often as you need to. For some of you, it will be harder to Ask for help. For others, you will struggle to Embrace awkward. I cannot begin to know how long each step will take for each one of you or how often you will need to repeat this grieving process. Again, there is no rule of thumb for this. Take your time: you will know when you have successfully unlocked each stage of grief and when you are able to move to the next step. Don't be discouraged by this. Grief is not a race. Take as long as you need at each step—no one is timing you.

Grief-o-Meter

It helps me to have the word DREAM and the five associated stages of grief memorized so that I can determine where I am on the "grief-o-meter." Grief-o-meter is just a funny word I made up so that I could figure out where I was in my healing. Grief is not as cut-and-dry as these categories would suggest, but they give me a general idea of what stage I am in and what I need to do to unlock the grief of that stage.

Here are some questions to help you process through the grief and get into the flow of healing:

Dare to Dream. Am I able to trust God to deliver me through this grief and into healing? Can I dare to dream that God can get me through this nightmare? Daring to Dream unlocks denial.

Remove the Stinger. Have I been able to identify what, if anything continues to sting me? Has the stinger been removed so that I can begin to heal? Removing the Stinger unlocks anger.

163

Embrace Awkward: Am I courageous enough to be comfortable with being uncomfortable? Change has happened to me, but am I allowing change to happen in me? Embracing Awkward unlocks sadness.

Ask for Help: Am I able to ask for what I need from God, friends, family, and myself? Can I be honest with myself and others and ask for the help I need? Asking for Help unlocks bargaining.

Move On: Am I able to accept what has happened to me, and move on as a person who has been changed for the better by what I have been through? Am I bitter or better? Moving On locks in acceptance.

If you reach the end of DREAM and you are having trouble moving on, you will know there is still some more healing that needs to happen. You will need to scan through the stages again and you may need to give more energy to one step in particular. Maybe you are not daring to dance and it is holding up your progress. Maybe you have done a great first round of medicine, but you need another dose of grief relief. DREAM and repeat. DREAM again. Go through the DREAM process as often as needed. DREAM again and again and again. Eventually you will be able to fully move on.

Triggers

Triggers are those unsolicited prompts that remind you of the past. Triggers can be different for each person and each grief. Triggers can be positive or negative. Because my husband was a pilot, there are obvious triggers for me to remember him: planes flying in the sky, going to an airport, and most assuredly, seeing a man in his airline uniform. Mike was also a runner, so when I see runners on the road – especially if they are wearing yellow – I miss him. These are all positive triggers and bring up fond memories of him but they can also trigger sadness because I miss him or anger that he is not here with me.

Other positive triggers that are not as obvious or predictable for me are smelling wood burning outside, seeing someone with hiking boots like he wore, or noticing a food he enjoyed in the grocery store. These pop up unannounced and bring him to mind.

Triggers that bring up negative memories are also unpredictable. Hearing an ambulance or driving past certain restaurants to can make me blue.

What makes triggers tricky is that you can't plan for them because they are usually spontaneous. A song on the radio, the smell of perfume, a toy she played with, an engagement party, or an invitation to a baby shower. Triggers come out of nowhere. You may find that as you are healing a trigger can bring up feelings you weren't aware you had. That's normal. Some simple investigation will let you know if this trigger is causing you to jump to the denial, anger, sadness, or bargaining stage of grief and if you are struggling with acceptance of the loss or longing. Use your keys appropriately. Dare to dream.

Thankfulness for the Journey

I can only go as fast, and as far, as I am able. There are times I wish I could grow faster or further. I grow impatient and frustrated with myself. But growth is a process that takes time and maturity, and you cannot rush maturity. Much patience and loving care is required in order for the soul to continue to develop, so I have to pace myself.

The soul takes its own sweet time to ripen. The best advice I can offer in the care of your spirit is to be gentle. Be kind to yourself. Allow yourself the dignity to find your own rhythm and stay in step with it. Listen to your heart and honor it above all else. You will find your way. You are being guided by the Great Spirit. Follow the way of your own life path.

Live Your Life

Your life will have its own calling. You have a unique purpose. Be true to your deepest self, because you have this one life to live, this one day to make a difference. You have this one moment to make a lasting and eternal impression. Our lives are like fossils imbedded in rock: we all leave our mark on this Earth. What do you want to be remembered for when the breath has left your body? Do those things that bring honor to memory. Be careful to not get caught up in the chaos and confusion of fast and furious living. Be deliberate and intentional in your choices.

Respect the Maker of life and seek His heart. Slow yourself down enough to hear His wisdom. Be aware of the constant connectedness you have to your Creator and allow Him to re-create you every day. Give God permission to work at will in your life to bring fresh thought and insight. Ask Him to enter your heart, invade your mind, and penetrate your will with His heart and mind and will. Pray for the Almighty to give you new strength through His power. Invite the Father to lead your family and bless your friends. Thank God for His ability to heal you and for His willingness to be ever-present with you. Remember that He, the Timeless One, will always be with you and never forsake you.

Be grateful for His wild graciousness to you. Be thankful for all the resources He provides for you. Appreciate the supply of life, love, and laughter. We receive gifts from The Giver that make our lives rich and meaningful and even joyful; give thanks for what The Eternal One has done, what He is doing, and what He will do.

Beloved Grievers, as we crest the hill and walk the final steps up out of the valley, I want to thank you for allowing me to journey alongside you. I thank you for traveling with me down these crooked CROSSroads. I will continue to pray for you and I humbly ask that you pray for me.

We will never forget the valley, but I love to see the wide-open spaces of grace stretched out before us. Journey on, my friend. Launch into the life that has been given to you, gifted to you. Continue to be brave. Believe in the Life-Giver and continue to commit your spirit to Him: God has much more to show you. Always remember that grief gives way to grace.

Even though we part ways, know that I will carry you in my heart. Your presence has been courage to me. I will pray that the Lord continues to bless you, grow you, expand your horizons, and enlarge your heart. And when our paths cross again, know that I will delight to see you.

Prayer for DREAM Again

Gracious God and Father,

You are the Almighty. You are the source of all life eternal. To You be praise, glory, honor, majesty, dominion, and power. Now and forever more.

Remove our loneliness and bless us with Your overwhelming presence. Bestow Your everlasting joy upon us. Call out to our dry bones to come alive. Command depression, despair, disease, and dysfunction to submit to Your authority. May we exchange our mourning for Your gladness. We lay down our defeat and discouragement to pick up Your praise.

Display Your glory before us, God. Sign Your faithfulness over our lives. Reveal Your majesty to us. Convey Your compassion for us. Write Your wishes across our minds. Tattoo Your love on our hearts. Stitch Your grace into our souls. Impress Your power into our palms. Send Your life down into our spirits. We are completely lifeless without You. You are Life. You are Love. You are Light. Replace our dreams with Your DREAM. May it be so.

Chapter 7

Dear DREAM Team:
Notes to the Supporter

Dear DREAM Team,

I call you the DREAM Team because you are obviously awesome and I appreciate you helping our grievers DREAM!!! This is a time in their lives that can feel more like a nightmare and they will need your help to Dare to DREAM. Thank you for loving this DREAMer enough to be a support person as they grieve. You can be a tremendous blessing in their lives when they need it the most. Whether they are grieving a loss or grieving something that they long for, know that your support and compassion are more valuable than you can imagine.

What do I mean by being a support person to the griever? Does that mean that you will understand and agree with all the choices of the griever? Certainly not. I don't know any two people who agree on everything.

What you can agree with, or agree to, is that you will love them and support them in ways that honor the process they are going though.

Think of a two-year-old. Not that grievers act like two-year-olds—well, maybe sometimes we do—but think of that two-year-old. That child is exploring and going after whatever they can get their grasping hands on. As infants, they would just lie around looking at their hands or playing in their bouncy chair. Now, these toddlers want to go on the swings, down the slides, and hold their own popsicle. Does the mom get mad at the toddler who wants to do all these things? No, she understands it is natural for this phase of development to want to explore and assert independence. She does not scold and shame the child for wanting to do these things, because she understands that it is a natural part of this growth phase. The mom places appropriate limits, and helps the child to learn and grow in a loving, safe environment.

Maybe grieving is like being a toddler. Grievers, like toddlers, are going through a huge life transition. We are both learning new skills every day. We get tired and need naps, but we fight the rest, because we want to be BIG! We want to get through this phase of growing or grieving as fast as possible! But it takes time, lots of patience, and continued learning and exploring. In order to be a support person to the griever, you need to realize all the changes that are happening to them simultaneously. Give them grace, because they are trying as hard as possible to get through this awkward stage.

Major Life Change

There must be some kind of natural transition that happens when we are grieving. Like the "terrible twos" or teenager years or mid-life change, growing is awkward. Grieving is uncomfortable, and grievers make mistakes. We are trying to figure out who we are now that so many things have changed. We have changed and we are still changing. I think the best way to support a griever starts with knowing that they are going through a major life transformation. Just as the two-year-old does not know how to hold a popsicle without getting it down the front of their shirt and in their hair and even on your clean shorts, grief is messy.

Allow the griever room to be messy for a while. Understand they may not know how to be smooth in social settings. Give them grace when they get their mess on you. They are doing the best they can; don't scold them and shame them for not knowing how to handle all of this. Just be compassionate, and maybe even offer to help them clean up the mess. Tell them how you are proud of them for trying new things and exploring and growing. Make sure they know how much you love them, even when they are a mess. You might even tell them they look cute with orange popsicle all over their face, or laugh with them when they realize what a big mess they have made.

Here are some examples of supporters who helped me in the healing process. See if there are a few tips you can pick up in how to help your friend or family member that is grieving.

Friend of the Year

My best friend Michele has been amazing! I call her "Friend of the Year." She is the kind of person who you don't even need to ask to help. She knows me well enough and cares deeply enough that she just does it. Michele's greatest support is in helping me find the humor when grief threatens to steal my funny bone. Michele listened to me rant and took me out for margaritas when needed. She texted to check on me several times daily. Michele helped me sort through bills and do my taxes and has really loved on my girls. She was sure to show up with a smile and jumped in to help without a complaint. She worked tirelessly to help me and even stuck by my side the whole day at my daughter's wedding when I needed her most. She has been a true friend and I could not thank her enough for all she has done for me. Michele is truly "Friend of the Year."

Singles Boot Camp

Wendy is another one of my best friends and I affectionately refer to her as "Wendy the Good Witch." Wendy is one of those dear people to whom I can tell anything and she doesn't even flinch. She is a true supporter and has a wealth of encouragement. She is not afraid to "go there" and she tackles the emotional load of grieving with me. Wendy takes me to lunch and asks, "How are you doing, really?" I don't have to pretend and we can cut through to the core of my pain and give it grace and love. She is a strong believer in me, and a source of such courage. She believes in me and I need that when I am feeling run over by grief.

Wendy is also a single lady and she has put me through what I call "single boot camp." After years of being married, my skills at being a single lady had gone into remission. Wendy models to me the necessary skills of navigating the social scene as a strong, independent woman. I am learning how to interact with single men in a positive way and I am actually learning how to flirt again. Well, maybe…I am still in training, but I am making progress. These things take time.

Spiritual Guide

Jeanne is a new friend who I met after Mike died and she has been an enormous help to me. Jeanne is a spiritual guide and she has assisted hundreds of people in developing their spiritual side. She prays for me and encourages me and helps me to tap into the Spirit like no one else I have ever met. Jeanne has a connection to God that challenges me to dig deeper in my faith and pursue this next phase in my life without fear! She speaks truth to me and instills in me the value of quiet time with God. Jeanne has been a Godsend and I am forever changed for knowing her tender heart.

Jeanne is also a massage therapist and gives the best massages I have ever had. Grief is hard on the body: muscles tense and stress builds up. When Mike died, I made a commitment to take care of myself and to not let stress get the best of me. I see Jeanne on a regular basis for massage and spiritual pep talks.

My Three Angels

These ladies are affectionately called "My Three Angels." The three of them have been friends for years and they have servant hearts, each one of them! Rachel, Cheryl, and Jen came over and helped me sort through piles of stuff that we had accumulated over the years. My workroom was full of items that were appropriate for our household before my husband died. Our goal was to pare down to the items I would need to move forward after death entered our home. They helped me determine what I needed to keep to rebuild my new life.

It was quite an undertaking and they helped with their positive attitudes and willingness to do whatever I needed them to do. They organized shelves, carted out unwanted items to their cars, and removed the clutter so that I could breathe again. Visual clutter clutters the mind and I needed clarity. I needed to eliminate unnecessary things from my workroom, which was a symbol of my life, and be left with only what I needed to go on into the future God had for me.

These same ladies also catered and served at my daughter Abbi's graduation party. Abbi graduated eight months after Mike died and these ladies continued their dedication to serving us. Like I said, they have beautiful servant hearts.

"Wine Down" Ladies

Once a month, my Wine Down Ladies would meet at someone's house and just hang out. No agenda. No sales pitch. Just pure friendship. These women are friends who have been there for me on this emotional roller coaster of grief. Laughter is healing to me and these women have provided lots of laughter. The consistency of seeing them once a month provided a rhythm that my grieving heart needed. They were sure to give me lots of hugs, tissues, and of course, wine.

Bible Study Girls

When all around me felt like it was changing it became extremely important for me get together with other women and find some normalcy. We met weekly for Bible study and prayer. I have learned from so many messed up people in the Bible that God loves us, not in spite of our messes, but because of our messes.

The Power of Presence

This strange story is an illustration of what I call "The Power of Presence." Your presence has power. Do not underestimate this power in the life of a griever. So many people are afraid to talk to those who have had a loss. "What do I say to them?" Don't say anything...just be with them (see the story of "Monkey Buddies" in Chapter 4).

First of all, there is nothing you can say to remove the profound pain they are experiencing, so don't try.

Secondly, what grievers need to know is that they are not alone in their pain. Your presence makes a difference.

Third, and lastly, most people say the wrong thing anyway to grievers. You are better off not saying a word. Hug them. Rub their shoulders. Get them a drink or snack. Listen to them. Do anything, but resist the urge to talk.

Silence is Gold

I had to remind myself of this recently when I met a woman at church who had just experienced a death in the family. I wanted to tell her that my husband died and I knew what she was going through. But telling her that I was grieving would only add to her grief...and how presumptuous of me to pretend to know what she was going through!

When Mike died, I can't tell you how many people tried to console me by telling me about when their brother died or when their mom died of cancer or their twin died when they were little. I don't mean to sound cold and heartless, but I was up to my eyeballs in heartache. The last thing I needed to hear about was more grief. I was already drowning in grief and they were pouring it on. These people did not mean to add to my grief. They did the best they could. I say this to you, so that you will be better informed the next time you are talking to someone in the throes of grief.

Do not add to their anguish by sharing your horror stories. Again, I don't say this to hurt you. Your sorrow is just as important as theirs. I am just asking you to be aware of their pain and not add more sadness to them.

Insult to Injury

Back to the story of me talking to the woman at church who was grieving. If I had not been so freshly aware of this dynamic from my own life, I would have vaulted off of this woman's misery and added insult to injury by telling her about my sad story. Better to keep my mouth shut and my ears open. I had to consciously close my lips and open my heart so that I didn't say a word about me and just keep the focus on her.

This is not a hard-and-fast rule. There is a time and place for everything and at some point I may talk to this woman again and be led to share my story. But this is a gentle reminder: grievers need to be heard more than they need to hear what you have to say.

Close Your Mouth, Open Your Heart

The old adage "if you can't say something nice, don't say anything at all" applies here. If you can't show up with a blessing, then certainly don't show up with your cursing. If you don't agree with decisions the griever is making, then, let me say this as gently as I can...shut your mouth and open your heart. Do not pass judgment on the griever. Do not say out loud to others, "Do you believe what he is doing?" If you must speak, speak only to God. Tell God your concerns and pray for the griever. Ask God to give the griever wisdom and guidance during this precarious time. If you disagree with a choice they are making, then ask God to help the griever learn in their own time. Do not withhold love from the griever. Do not send your curse on their choices; only send blessings for continued courage and learning.

Let Them Have the Floor

The problem with talking to grievers about your experience is that you can make it about you and your grief then. In reality, it is not about you, it is about them. So let them do the talking. Let them have the gift of you listening to their grief. Do not spoil it by stealing the show. Out of respect for their loss or longing, let them have the floor.

I hope you are able to track what I am trying to communicate here. Bottom line, show up and shut up. Your face is what they need to see. And if you must talk, say something nice about the person that passed. Tell them how much you loved Aunt Nancy's beautiful house, or how much you will miss Mike's hugs, or how you loved Frank's sense of humor. Say something that compliments their dearly departed.

It is also nice to hear that you are sorry for their pain. Tell them you will keep them in your thoughts and you will continue to pray for them. Grievers need these kinds of comments. Whatever you do, don't say it must be God's will, or God must have needed another angel, or it was just their time. These are cliché and rather cold. Again, hear me on this: less talking and more listening. Better to say less and hug more.

Okay? So, the next time you go to a funeral or run into someone in the grocery and they start telling you their story of loss or longing, I hope you will remember what I have told you and look them in the eyes. Reach out and touch their hand. Hug them. Tell them you are sorry for their pain, then close your mouth and open your heart. I think you will both be blessed.

Fragile

My warning when you want to critique the griever takes a different tone. This is my warning label to you: FRAGILE! HANDLE WITH CARE! DO NOT TAMPER! Do not even begin to presume that you have any right to judge, condemn, or criticize the griever. Even if they are not meeting your expectations, and are making choices that you do not agree with, your job is to be a support to them. There is never a time in the grieving process that you are allowed to put on your judge's robe and pound out your beliefs on them. However, there maybe a time when it would be appropriate to step in and guide them to the help they need. If they are in danger of physically hurting themselves or others, they are extremely fragile. Please remember it is vital to treat them with love and compassion while pointing them to the help they need. No circumstance warrants you the position of critic.

At no point are you allowed to hold court and decide if you think their choices are right or wrong, even if they are wrong. You will only be compounding the griever's grief. What they need from you, and what they have a right to expect from you as friends or family members, is respect. Respect for how hard it must be to be knocked to your knees and not know how to approach life again. Respect for trying to manage life and grief in the same breath. Respect for their efforts to learn how to walk over the hot coals of pain and heartache. Respect.

Give Courage

If I can be so bold as to speak to your heart: you do not have the right to judge anyone else, no matter what they are doing. You do not have a position on a throne that allows you to condemn another person. You, yourself, are human, too. Your only job is to encourage. Encourage means to give courage. Discourage means to take courage from someone else. Do you really want to take someone's courage from their heart? Do not discourage the griever. They need all the courage you can give them. Give courage.

Suggestions of Ways to Help

Here is a list of ways to help grievers that are practical and helpful. That first month after an event (death, divorce or accident), grievers are bombarded by the "3 C's"...cards, casseroles, and carnations. What else can we do for them on an ongoing basis? What do they need that we can provide?

- Take out the trash
- Pick up prescriptions
- Drop off groceries
- Yard work
- Clean out fridge - remember the casseroles?
- Handyman tasks
- Clean their house
- Babysit
- Teach them to pay bills, do taxes, or other bookkeeping tasks
- Drive them to run errands

- Take them to coffee
- Buy a gift certificate for a massage or mani/pedi
- Car maintenance
- Take them to exercise
- Do their laundry

This is a simple list of suggestions on how to help grievers and support them in their healing process. The best way to find out how to help your specific griever is to ask them directly. If they are not quite sure what to ask for you can give them some ideas from this list. Maybe something will prompt them to know what would help. Of course, there are many more ideas that you will think of so please use them as appropriate. We are all learning together.

Just like every griever is an individual, every support person is also an individual. Don't feel like you need to make a gourmet meal if you don't know how to cook (or don't like to cook). If you are allergic to trees don't feel guilty that you can't rake their leaves. This is meant to be a mutually beneficial activity and a blessing to you as the support person as much as it is a blessing to the griever. You both will feel good about this if you stay in your gift mix. My sister is an amazing apple pie baker and I was more blessed by her delivering a fresh, warm pie than anything else she could have done for me. Stay in your gift set and your support will be a true gift.

My deepest thanks to you for stepping in and stepping up to help this griever. Know that your thoughtfulness will be part of their healing process. Your smile, hug, text, and prayers are real medicine to help relieve their grief.

Whether your friend is grieving from a loss or a longing I assure you that kindness is always appreciated. I am praying for you as you are praying for them.

Dare to DREAM,

Kristi